NAVIGATING MILITARY LIFE WITH INTENTION AND GRACE

ADRIANNE AMUNDSON

WESTBOW
PRESS®
A DIVISION OF THOMAS NELSON
& ZONDERVAN

WestBow Press books may be ordered through booksellers or by contacting:

WestBow Press
A Division of Thomas Nelson & Zondervan
1663 Liberty Drive
Bloomington, IN 47403
www.westbowpress.com
1 (866) 928-1240

ISBN: 978-1-6642-0050-0 (sc)
ISBN: 978-1-6642-0051-7 (hc)
ISBN: 978-1-6642-0049-4 (e)

Library of Congress Control Number: 2020914001

Print information available on the last page.

WestBow Press rev. date: 9/2/2020

To David, Thank you for believing in me and for encouraging me to walk and live out my dreams daily!

CONTENTS

INTRODUCTION

Grace is defined as elegance or beauty in what you do and say. As I read this definition and think about military life, my first thought is that they don't go together. This life is filled with so much that's not easy to navigate, often because things are constantly changing, like homecoming dates, deployment leave dates, work hours, when and where you're moving, you have to say, "See you later," to great friends, and so much more. Encountering any of the items on this list makes it challenging to be gracious as you live life in the military.

Intentional is one of my most favorite words and actions. Intention is defined as being mindful in your actions and words. If I could pick one word I want to live my life by, it's this. Intentional.

When you get knocked down, which can happen often in military life with all the unexpected changes and being without your spouse for such extended periods of time, it's hard not to throw in the towel and not even try. Because when you try to be intentional, the plan always seems to get foiled.

Going through life can feel like going through the motions, even more so when life throws challenges at you. But what if you did it with grace and intention? What if you changed your perspective? Do you believe you could change the script?

The military has a grip on your life because your spouse signed on the dotted line and it's the nature of the job, but through this life blessings overflow, lifelong friendships are created, and you have experiences no one else does. It's easy to let this life tear you down, make you want to stay locked up at home, but there can also be a way to navigate it with joy and purpose.

Through my story, I'd like to navigate making the most of this life with you.

Before starting, please know this, my story *will* be different than yours. My hope and prayer is that through my words and my story, you are encouraged and inspired to live out your life, whatever the circumstances may be, with gratitude, intention, and grace.

ONE

WHERE IT ALL BEGAN

Our Story

Recently, I sat in my kitchen during the quiet early hours of the morning reflecting.

As I stared out the window, I was missing my husband David, who was gone on what we call "work trips." This particular morning, all the memories about when David and I first met and how we spent much of our time together flooded in.

Our story begins in 5th grade.

A tall, handsome boy walked into my 5th grade class halfway through the year.

Spoiler alert. That tall, handsome boy—it was David! But I'm sure you already knew that. Of course, I didn't know at the time, or even dream in the years that followed that he would still be in my life today.

The day he first came into our class is a memory that still plays in my head, and a day I will never forget. The moment he walked in, I leaned over, elbowed my friend, and whispered, "He's so cute!" And so it began.

Walking home from school was a thing back when David and I were in upper elementary. On that first day we met, our teacher asked if I would walk home with him. I learned that we only lived three houses away from each other. This girl over here was grinning, thinking it was meant to be!

For this young 5th grader and her understanding of life at that age, it felt like love at first sight. Well, love or simply becoming all googly eyed for a ten-year-old. It was in that first moment I saw him that he gave me butterflies, but it wouldn't be the only time. He still gives me butterflies!

Friendship

As I looked out the back window of my dream kitchen not too long ago, the basketball hoop caught my eye. It holds a special place in my heart.

We spent many afternoons shooting hoops, playing 2-on-2 with our brothers, playing H-O-R-S-E and P-I-G, and having conversation after conversation. Our friendship grew right there, at a basketball hoop in the driveway of my parents' house.

We haven't been out to shoot hoops much since we've moved into our house, but when the weather is warmer, it's game on! And you better believe it will always bring me back to those wonderful memories of where the story or our life together began.

This was the beginning of a friendship that continued through elementary, middle, and high school. Our neighbors joked that we liked each other, you know that young kind of crush, and should date. We always laughed it off and didn't actually date for quite a few years. Although I never knew if David felt the same way, just laughing it off because I did. Perhaps I should ask him.

Truth be told, I didn't think we ever would go on a date. We spent many afternoons outside playing stickball or basketball with our brothers. We hung out at our neighbors' house together, dressed up in silly costumes, went to youth group and on mission trips, all as friends and nothing more.

Time passed and as freshmen in high school we actually went out on our first date. It was a group date, you know the ones where you go with your friends, but there are unspoken couples. It was a one and done date for the time being. David was quiet and didn't talk about it and I guess I got cold feet, but it was enough of an impression to remember. The movie we saw that day was *Shrek*, so that movie will always hold a special place in my heart.

Days went back to usual after that date, almost like it never happened. We still sat and ate lunch together, but spending time together at the house shooting hoops was becoming less frequent.

We attended the same youth group and had the opportunity to go on a mission trip together. While on the trip, in one of the final evenings after leaving chapel time, David pulled me aside and asked if he could talk to me. Okay sure, I thought, not having a clue about what he was about to say. We laid on a basketball court, staring up at the stars and watching bats fly overhead at the orphanage where we served, and talked about life and our relationship. So romantic, right?

He said he felt like we were drifting apart and missed the time we spent together when we were younger, mostly before high school. I honestly was a little caught off guard that this was where our conversation would go.

You must know, if you are reading this and don't know us personally, that I was and probably still am, much more outgoing than David. I was involved in sports and David wasn't. He was very quiet in high school, keeping to himself and his group of friends. So, I chalked up his feelings of us drifting apart to the busyness of all I was involved in at school and the extracurricular activities.

We agreed we would try to hang out more, but without scheduling anything, we didn't get in extra time together.

Fast forward a year or so and it was high school graduation time. Our lives were going different directions. David had enlisted in the Navy and was getting ready to leave for boot camp, and I was enjoying my summer, working at Baskin Robbins and then gearing up to head off to college.

On the day before he left for boot camp, he asked me to lunch one last time. This would be the first time we went out just the two of us, and the first time we went on a "date" since that group date our freshman year of high school.

It's funny the details you remember from some of these events. He drove us to a Mexican restaurant nearby, where we sat in a booth by the window. During lunch we had a normal conversation about what we each had going on in our life, but then as we finished eating and were getting ready to leave, David pulled out a stack of short little letters he had journaled to me.

I didn't know what to think. I didn't read the letters while we sat across the booth from each other, but tucked them away until I got home. I couldn't wait to get to my house, open the letters up, and read them. Even though I was excited to get home to read the letters, I also didn't want our time together to end. This would be the last time I would see David before he shipped off to boot camp bright and early the next morning, and there was no telling what the future held. All of the sudden it felt like there just wasn't enough time. It felt like a cliff-hanger I wasn't expecting just a few hours before.

Curled up on my bed, I sat in my room reading those letters and was somewhat surprised about his feelings about our relationship. Butterflies filled my stomach again. The reality set in that he was leaving for boot camp the next day and there was so much I wanted to talk about but time wasn't on our side. Oh, how this was foreshadowing for what was to come and feeling like time was never on our side, thanks to the military.

That summer unfolded in a way I never expected. My heart

longed to see David again and spend time with him. The next best thing was staying in touch through old-fashioned handwritten letters. Getting mail was never so exciting!

Not a day went by that I wouldn't run down to the mailbox, checking to see if there was another letter. Some days there would be multiple and other days, none. Some days a letter marked #3 would come in the mail before #1 and #2. The wait (oh, the wait!) to get the rest of those letters. We can all agree that getting a letter or package in the mail is worthy of making our day, right?

My heart would skip a beat each time my name, written in David's handwriting, was on an envelope waiting for me in the mailbox.

One summer afternoon, everything changed. My phone rang. The caller ID showed up as "Unknown," which I often would ignore. I was hesitant to pick up the phone and answer this call, but something told me to answer. Boy, oh boy, am I so glad I answered because on the other end was the sweet and soothing voice of the man that I was falling more and more in love with each passing day. I was again filled with butterflies knowing it was really David on the other end of the line.

Some of those memorable moments, the details are clear as day, and other times I was so wrapped up in the moment that the details are clear as mud. All I remember are the feelings I had. This phone call was definitely the latter. I can't tell you much of what our conversation was about or how long we were able to talk, but I can remember where I was sitting in my house (such a strange detail to remember, I know!) and the topic of his upcoming graduation. David mentioned when graduation was and that he had only three tickets.

Three. He has many more people in his family than three and who was I, the girl from next door, the friend from childhood, that I would get to claim one of those coveted tickets? Yet, without hesitation, I asked, "Can I come?"

He was quick to say, "Yes!" Maybe even relieved that I asked.

Looking back now, I wonder how I convinced my parents to let me go. But we did know their family and I would be traveling and staying with David's dad and brother. So off to Chicago I went. I'm so honored to say that I have been there with David since the beginning of this whole military journey we are now doing together.

The trip to Chicago was fabulous, and seeing David again only set the butterflies in motion. The time to see and spend with David was short because he was being sent off to more schooling for his job in the Navy. Our plans, if we had any defined plans, were interrupted day two when hurricanes were forecasted in Florida, where David was headed next, and he would be leaving a day earlier than expected. My heart sank at this news. I wasn't ready to say, "See you later," at least not yet. When would I see him again? Again, there was so much to say and yet we didn't have time.

David's dad, brother, and I still had one more day before our flight headed back home, so we were going to make the most of our time on that day we no longer had with David. We headed out to explore the Shed Aquarium. While sitting and eating in the cafeteria, I got a message that David was at the airport and we could come and spend some time with him before he left. There was no question about whether we would go or not and headed over to the airport right away. We passed through security and sat in the terminal with a sea of other sailors saying a final "see you later" to their loved ones before they too were off to their next destination.

Before he boarded, David gave me another envelope filled with words that would melt my heart. The envelope was thick, so I knew he must have taken a good bit of time writing the night before.

I held that letter close and waited to open and read it until I was alone in my hotel room that night. I sat on the bed reading his heart poured out over those pages and just cried. I cried because I missed him. I cried because the feelings of love were growing and so real. I cried because I didn't know when I would see him again. And I cried because, well . . . I am a crier!

He is great with his words and knows just how to make a girl feel loved. Now I need to go dig up those letters and read them again. Just thinking about reading these again get my heart all giddy and excited!

The best news going forward was that boot camp was over, so many restrictions lifted, and now he had his cell phone again. It seems so small and simple, but it felt huge. There was no more memorizing my phone number to be able to call. No more waiting until a certain day or time. No more calling from a public phone. No more having to wait for the mail to reach him.

Phone calls were daily and long. I have no clue what we talked about that kept us on the phone, but we wanted to spend as much time together as we could and, being thousands of miles apart, this is how we did it. Sometimes I wonder how I kept up with all my college homework.

In a new relationship, even though we had already known each other so long at this point, there was still newness and mystery about each other. I loved learning about what made him tick and the things he was passionate about.

At this point in our story, David and I still considered each other friends. There was no other label on our relationship. It of course felt like more but at this point, neither him nor I asked or wanted to burst the bubble.

I remember the day we finally had a conversation about our relationship. It was another one of those milestone moments that has left its mark—in a good way, of course. It was October 10, 2004. I think I asked something along the lines of, "are we dating?"

We are so romantic . . . not! (Just wait for the proposal story.) He responded with an "I guess," and we moved forward with no more words about it. It felt strange to talk to people about him and call him my boyfriend after so many years of being friends.

But, there it was, we decided simply. This kind of simplicity is still who we are today.

Our phone calls continued for quite some time while he was still in Florida and I was in Washington. We didn't know where he would be next, but the day of knowing what the next four years would hold drew closer.

At the time, the top of the class would get to pick orders first. David never enjoyed school, but this was important to him, so he put his best foot forward to be at the top of the class and get to choose first. Not only did he want to secure an early pick, but he worked to convince his classmates that Washington was a terrible place to be because it rained all the time.

Little did I know, this would be a big part of my future once we were married, waiting on pins and needles to hear where the military would send us.

The waiting felt like forever, but *the* phone call finally came. Our conversation was short and sweet. David is a no fluff kind of guy. Very matter of fact, David informed me he was coming back to Washington. He was coming *home*! We would finally have the chance to date in person instead of just over the phone. I was ecstatic and waited eagerly, or maybe not so eagerly, for him to get back. Being long distance up to this point, I'd be lying if I said there wasn't some nervousness about how it would go.

One day, he kept calling to see where I was and what I was doing. In college, my studies were priority number one and I wouldn't skip out on them. It was a 10:00 pm bedtime for me, and everyone knew not to come knock on my door after that forbidden time.

Not soon after he called, my sister, who went to the same college, called and invited me to her apartment for cookies. I politely declined because . . . studying! My sister and her roommate were relentless, continually calling me. When I wouldn't agree to come, they offered to just come and pick me up. At that point, annoyed and frustrated, I agreed. I had been studying in the lounge, so I headed back to my room, put away my notes and got ready to go when suddenly someone was knocking at my door. There were no peep holes on our dorm room doors, so who it was and why someone was knocking, I had no idea. It couldn't be my sister because she would be waiting for me in her car just outside the dorm lobby.

I opened the door. To my enormous surprise, standing in front of me was the tall, handsome man I had fallen in love with. My jaw dropped in shock. No words came out of my mouth and I wrapped my arms around him as tight as I could. I told him I was headed to my sister's apartment for cookies. David just laughed and let me in on the secret. That was only a ploy to get me in place for his surprise.

That may be the only time that he was able to surprise me! This far along in our military career, I ask far too many questions, and want to know *all* the details. The only way he will surprise me now is if he shows up earlier than expected.

Finally, we'd have time to spend together in person. It's at these times you realize how much you took for granted during the time you spent together before. Not a weekend went by we weren't together, either in Oak Harbor where he was stationed or up in Bellingham where I was going to school. The weekends suddenly became so much more exciting, even if it just meant hanging out in my dorm room or his barracks room. We were together and that's what mattered.

Being apart and spending the beginning of our relationship over the phone, there was great newness in time spent together, holding hands, kissing, and even saying, "I love you."

It was a quiet evening and we were sitting on the couch at his dad's house just talking. You know the scene from the movies. One person leans in and it happens. He will never let me forget that it was me who made the first move, but right after that was the first time he ever said "I love you!" The butterflies swarmed my stomach yet again that night and our relationship continued to grow.

Oh, how glad I am that he was able to convince everyone else not to take the orders to Whidbey Island because it rained all the time! It does rain a bit, but the views and scenery are breathtaking. Everything started right here, close to home. Funny thing, as I write this, we have orders to head back to Whidbey for a third tour. We've had two babies, bought our first house, and made so many memories there. Gearing up for another move back to Whidbey Island is beginning to feel a little like we are going back to where we started.

Dating and the Military

As a little girl, you dream about what life will be like when you get older. You dream about what you will be. You dream about who you will marry. You dream about having kids, how many you hope to have, and becoming a parent. But, did it ever occur to you that the man you marry and his job would have so much control on many aspects of life? I know I didn't.

Just like anything in life, I'm not sure you can be fully prepared for what's to come until you actually experience it.

I had no idea what all was involved in military life. None! When I started dating David, I quickly realized I had a lot to learn. Not having any family members in the military, everything was so foreign to me—and let me tell you, I was in for a rude awakening. And good thing I didn't listen when my family and friends questioned my ability to be a military spouse all those years ago.

The first time David left, we were dating, but I'd say our relationship at that point was serious. I was a mess—a *hot* mess! I cried *a lot*.

My emotions were strong and the struggle was hard, so much harder than I ever imagined. The days felt incredibly long and I'd be lying if I told you I handled it well. I didn't. There were days I didn't know how to function. Who knew one person could make you feel this way? I worried a lot. And those worries, want to know what they were about? David's safety. Looking back now, I see how unrealistic my worries were, but in the moment it felt so real.

Somehow in my sorrow, or perhaps guided by those close to me, I at least had the where-with-all to seek help. Help, you say? *Yes*! It was that serious and I felt that terrible every single day. I didn't realize or even fully appreciate it at the time, but now that I am older and wiser, I am so thankful for all the mentors who were able to speak love and truth into my life at just the perfect time.

The first phone call I made was to a dear friend, Brian, who happened to be both David's and my youth pastor just a few years prior. He knew us both well and I knew he could provide me a little bit of counseling, and even some tough love. The conversation left me feeling encouraged and better prepared to take on military life. In typical Adrianne style, I took notes, and those notes are still sitting in my Bible today. They serve as a reminder of the great advice I received that day, but also as a reminder of how far I have come.

That conversation with Brian was not the only one I would need during the first detachment.

The next phone call was a bit different. A dear friend and mentor listened to me share my fears and worries about David being gone. She happened to have a good friend, Cindy, who was a Marine spouse. She had almost twenty years of military spouse experience. That timeframe was something I could not fathom at the time. I'll never forget my conversation with her.

It just so happened the day Cindy called, David was on the ship, and I hadn't heard from him since he left about a week or so before. I was a wreck. My focus to get anything done, including studying, was few and far between. I probably paced the house most of the day, hoping my phone would ring. If only I had an iWatch counting my steps back then!

The conversation started out pretty innocent, just getting to know each other a little bit. She shared some of her story and we talked about my fears, the biggest of which was losing David while he was gone. I suppose that's most military spouses' worst nightmare during deployment.

The tone of the conversation changed with one single question. It was a question I needed to hear, but didn't want to even think about. The question about dropped me to my knees and brought a flood of uncontrollable tears. "What if he doesn't come back home?"

On the other end of the phone, I was almost angry she would even ask that. How dare she make me think about that, but the reality was there. What if he didn't, but what was the sense in worrying about the what-ifs?

Through the sobs, all I could get out was, "I don't know!" My worrying, my anxiety, was shining bright in that moment, and what better time to deal with it than right then. In the moment, I thought she was asking me this question to get under my skin, but I know better now. She was being my advocate, challenging me to address my feelings and opening my eyes to the miserable mess I had made this time without David. Sometimes, we just need someone to snap us out of our thoughts and take the reality of life head on. The what-ifs get us nowhere but into trouble.

She reminded me that I can't worry or stress the what-ifs. I learned that no news is good news and he was actually safe out on a big giant floating piece of steel. If I wanted peace and strength in this time apart, I needed to lean in and trust the Lord.

Are we ever one hundred percent safe, even here at home? No! There is always something that could happen. There will always be what-ifs, but if we live our life being held back from those things, we miss out on the goodness of life.

I'm so thankful for this conversation, for the truth she spoke, even when it was hard to hear, and her willingness to encourage me through a time I wasn't quite sure I would get through.

If you're a military spouse, can I just encourage you to find another spouse you can confide in and look up to? So often in this military life, we bottle up our emotions because we feel like society tells us we need to be strong, and can do this just fine alone. It can feel like we are the only one struggling with something, but hear me loud and clear—you, my friend, are not alone!

We *need* others to do life with. Others who can speak truth, love, and encouragement, into us, on the days that go well and especially on the days that don't. It doesn't take long to realize that military life is not ordinary, and those outside the military circle don't quite understand no matter how hard they try, but at no fault to them. Find a friend, a mentor, let them love you. I promise you, it's worth it!

I'm delighted to share with you that Cindy and I have connected again after many years since that conversation. I'm sure she wondered after our phone call how I would ever make it as a military spouse. How could she not, when even I did myself? I was so happy to share with her that we are almost fifteen years in and have overcome so many fears and obstacles I never imagined I'd have the strength to overcome. Her tough love was hard to hear and yet made an incredible and positive impact on the life that I live and the story I get to tell you.

Conversations with others during these first struggles with military life didn't always go as well as others.

I stood in the kitchen of the house I was renting with three college roommates, talking to my dad about how things were going. I was in tears. Life felt so hard, and I missed David more than words could express.

In his wisdom, and I'm sure not meaning to sound harsh, he says to me, "How are you going to survive as a military spouse if you just cry all the time?" The tears only flowed harder. Now I wasn't just sad, but angry. In between the sobs I answered him, "I'm allowed to cry!" I bet if I asked him now how he felt I was doing as a military spouse, he would be nothing but proud. I know my dad didn't mean to hurt me. He was being realistic and probably had no idea how to comfort his daughter over the phone that was so obviously struggling.

Over the years, my parents and family have come to better understand this military life and the tears, which still happen, a bit more.

You might be feeling this way too about your friends and family. It's a totally different life we live and it's easy for people, even those who love us the most, to tell us to just pull it together and deal with

13

it. I'm sure you've heard, "Well, you knew this when you chose to get married." This only makes it worse.

Friends who aren't military probably have good intentions, but this unfortunately doesn't help. Yes, we did know when we said "I do" that our spouses would deploy for long periods, but knowing and actually experiencing it are two different things. Nothing can prepare you for months on end apart from your spouse.

For those of you who are on the receiving end of these comments and lack of understanding of military life, share with your family what life is like. Be open and honest about how you are feeling. Allow them to ask questions. It's not a life you can understand unless you have lived it. Give grace to those who don't know and allow them in to learn more.

Those early days, first as a military girlfriend and then a young military spouse, were filled with learning and growing. Mentors urged me to get plugged in, so I did, even as David's girlfriend, because I wanted to show him that I cared. I just needed other people around me who understood what I was going through because it was foreign to those closest to me.

Other than not hearing from David often, or at least not often enough according to my standards, I battled eating regular meals. I could busy myself so much throughout the day that I forgot about eating, and no, I didn't even get hungry. I would wait for my roommates to get home to eat, or would call friends to come over and sit with me while I ate dinner, because eating alone wasn't happening.

A few times I would kindly invite myself over to other people's houses and ask if I could sit at their house while they went about their business. I would take my hot pocket with me (I've learned a lot about nutrition since then!), heat it up, and sit in the presence of someone else to eat. It sounds so silly, I know. I've tried to figure out why this was the case. I mean, it's totally opposite of most people's problem, right? This was emotional eating in the most backwards of ways. The only reason I can come up with for being this way . . .

loneliness. The quietness was absolutely paralyzing at the time. Life has changed now that I'm a mom.

This was all just the beginning to the story I am sharing with you over these next chapters. This life is far from easy, as I am sure you have gathered so far and will learn in the pages to come. Some say it gets easier, but I'm not so sure I agree because my experience tells me otherwise. More manageable, maybe, but easier, *no*! But— yes, there is a *but*—that handsome man I fell in love with all those years ago and the life we get to live together is one hundred percent completely worth it. I wouldn't want it any other way.

MY NAVY SAILOR

Becoming the Mrs.

The foundation of marriage is built on love, respect, and trust. You stand in front of all your family and closest friends, and gaze into each other's eyes acknowledging out loud the vows you will uphold in your marriage. Remember those? They aren't just something you say as part of the ceremony, but words to live by *daily*.

Not being married yet, I didn't have a network of other military spouses to lean on. I was a ball of worry as deployment number one approached.

My worries were all consuming. Would David still love me when he got back? Would he even make it back home? How was I going to go without him for so long? And on and on! Six months is a long time, and that's not even the longest of deployments.

Before this first deployment, we were either so head over heels for each other and our worlds revolved completely around one another, or we were wise at our ripe old age of twenty. I'm going to go with the latter of the two, because it makes me feel better. Somehow, I got the idea that we needed to write a "covenant" to each other, a list of things we promised each other while David was deployed and we couldn't be together. He agreed to do it without me having to persuade him or convince him why. I consider myself a lucky girl!

Those lists were written in 2005 and would you believe that I found them still saved to my computer? I'm not sure if that means I am a pack rat or am just that organized. I'll let you decide.

Before opening up the document to see what we wrote, I only could remember one item on that list, and it was the promise to never be with a person of the other gender alone—in a car, a room, etc. I know right now you might be thinking, *what?* It might sound crazy, but your mind can play dirty tricks on you while your spouse is gone, and temptation, even when no harm is intended, is always there trying to sneak in. I'd hoped that these covenants would keep us mindful of our commitment to one another.

If you've never experienced a deployment or time apart from your spouse, here is a little example of what I mean. You don't hear from your spouse for a day, which up until now you did. You get in your head telling yourself something's changed. You know it. You convince yourself they don't love you anymore and they've found someone else, in just one day. Ha! I know that thought sounds completely irrational, but I bet if you ask other military spouses, I'm not alone in experiencing these mind tricks.

You've heard the rumors of spouses cheating and the actuality of that happening is far greater than I'd like to admit. So, this thought of your spouse not being faithful while deployed after just one day of not hearing from him might sound a bit nuts, but the idea is not really that far-fetched.

The point of the whole covenant was similar to the vows you make when you get married. We were committed to each other, though we weren't yet married, and little did we know it was the beginning bricks to the solid foundation our marriage would become.

A little special treat for you, the lists we created so many years ago! David's list to me looked like this…

Adrianne, I promise you that:

1. *I will always love you.*
2. *I will always respect and trust you.*
3. *I will never let divorce become an option.*
4. *I will always do my best to communicate with you.*
5. *I will always turn to you first when I have a problem.*
6. *I will never be alone with another woman.*
7. *I will always try my best to keep our best interests in my mind when I am making decisions.*

And mine, like this…

David, I promise you that:

1. *I will be loyal to you always, when we are together, and especially when we are apart.*
2. *I will respect you.*
3. *I will never be alone in a room or car with another man.*
4. *I will not allow male friends to cross the line or rely on them as my biggest support while you are gone.*
5. *Divorce will never be an option.*
6. *I will always do my best to communicate with you.*
7. *I will do my best not to worry.*

As much as we tried to prepare ourselves for deployment, to put in place those things to remind us of each other on the bad days, what was coming was still going to be hard. You just can't prepare yourself for what it will feel like to not have your other half right there when you need them.

Deployment was coming and David decided what better way to kick off the deployment than a proposal. I'm not sure if this made things easier or harder.

We spent as much time as we could together before it was time to say, "See you later," for way longer than I would ever want. I remember right around that time we went for a walk around the neighborhood where we both grew up. Both our parents were still living there. As we walked, he kept fumbling in his pocket. He seemed distracted. I asked multiple times if something was wrong, but the answer was always the same, "Nothing!"

A few weekends later we were together and he had slipped the ring under his pillow. All was good until I reached under him and his pillow to give him a hug. There was something with a soft smooth cover and the shape of a square. I pulled my hand out from under the pillow and quickly asked, "What is that?"

He looked at me, laughed a little, and said, "Why do you have to ruin everything?"

You see, the evening before, we went to dinner in Seattle. After dinner, we took our cheesecake to go and headed downtown by the water. Well, remember the worry business that so easily overcomes me? It happened again. It was dark and there were people parked a little ways away and I started to worry they were going to, oh I don't know, attack us or something crazy. He tried to get me to calm down, but I think my telling him over and over, while also becoming more panicked, convinced him to finally give in and head back home. What I didn't know was he was planning to propose down by the water. Oops!

Well, the secret was out now, and I may have guilted him that weekend as we were getting ready to say our goodbyes in my room at college that evening. "You're not going to make me wait a whole other week are you???"

Right there in my room, as I sat on my bed, he got down on his knee and with the ring box open asked the question every girl dreams of hearing. "Will you marry me?"

I blurted out a very quick *yes*!

With all the excitement of being engaged, perhaps it took away some of the anxiety and tension associated with having to say, "See you later," all too soon.

Those feelings of anxiousness were still inevitable for me. For those experiencing it for the first time, and maybe every time, a deployment of three, four, five, six, or more months away from the person you love so dearly is impossible to fathom.

The last two weeks or so for me always feel like trying to fit in and soak up six plus months' worth of time and memories together. I get frustrated when another evening comes to an end, another day closer to that dreaded day. At this point, time just feels like it's running out, but then at the same time you're ready for them to just go already so the ticker starts counting down the days for them to be back in your arms again. It's a brutal battle of emotions.

Speaking of crazy emotions before deployment, let's add planning a wedding. Sounds like a great idea, right?

Looking back at it now, somehow I remained relatively calm and hopeful with all the uncertainty of his schedule and that he would actually be home *and* off work to stand at the altar with me and become husband and wife.

David and I were engaged for less than a month before he shipped out on a six-month deployment. We looked ahead a little bit, but not too far, to pick a date because who knew how long the window would be once he got home from deployment before having to ship back out again. We picked a date that will forever be special—December 21.

I know what you're thinking. *Are you crazy? Right before Christmas?* Our families had their thoughts about our date too. It was too cold, too close to Christmas, and *how about you just wait for summer?* But they didn't know military life. They didn't know the uncertainty of how plans could change in an instant. And let me tell you, I'm so glad we stuck with what we wanted because, had we waited, well, I bet you can guess what would have happened.

Yes, that's right, he was gone again and the summer wedding they wanted wouldn't have happened.

Being young and engaged, we learned quickly we would need to make decisions for ourselves, and take with a grain of salt the input from others because they didn't know or understand military life.

Before David left, we discussed getting married in the courthouse prior to deployment. As a young couple, it financially could have benefited us, especially just starting off, but when telling our family about it, they didn't seem to understand why we would want to do that. It would make our wedding not feel the same and so forth. It's a good thing we didn't join the military for the money, I guess!

While David was gone, I planned away. He got glimpses of what was coming when he got home but otherwise was pretty much out of the loop. Whether he liked it or not, he had to trust me with all the details because out on the ship, he was helpless and useless when it came to planning a wedding. Well, other than the simple no or yes, that is.

As the date grew closer to homecoming and the wedding, the pressure started to rise a little— eagerly awaiting his homecoming but also starting to wonder if he would really make it home. Wouldn't you know those dreaded words for anyone whose spouse is deployed were passed down. They'd been extended! I'm not sure we have ever been on a deployment where this didn't happen at least once. Now we just expect it, but back then, well, we were on a timeline.

Thankfully his extension was just a short two weeks, which wasn't much considering we had just spent six months apart. What's another week or two added on? It felt like a drop in the bucket.

Thankfully we had a little bit of a buffer with our wedding date and David made it home about a month before we walked down the aisle. There was a bit of a rush to get final details squared away, attend fittings for tuxes, and show David the venue because he hadn't seen it. I hoped he'd like it. If not, there wasn't much we could do to change it at that point.

Yes, our wedding anniversary is close to Christmas and we are often traveling or spending time with family on our special day, but I wouldn't change it for the world. With our rotation date during the holiday season, there's a good chance we will celebrate that day by walking into a new house for the first time. Funny how life changes over the years of marriage.

Saying I Do

Standing in front of our family, friends, and pastor that blustery winter day, it was nothing but joyful smiles, after the nerves wore off, of course. The stress leading up to that day had disappeared and there was nothing but joy as I imagined what life was going to be like from this day forward.

That day, all the loose ends came together in perfect timing as it always seems to when it comes to things in the military.

This man, who was first a stranger, then a good friend, eventually a boyfriend and inevitably my fiancé, would become my husband. It sounded so weird to call him that, yet was so exciting!

Looking back now, I'm not sure how I thought we were anywhere near old enough to start life out on our own. Many people around us were not shy in letting us know they thought we were too young. At that point, all that mattered was that we were together, and we would be together every night. The nights he was home anyway. It would be the start to an incredible adventure I couldn't wait to be on, but I still was completely naïve to what this military life would entail.

My life changed the moment I said, "I do," in more ways than I would ever imagine that day. Nothing—absolutely nothing—would prepare me for the life that began the day of our wedding. I was jumping into a life filled with so many unknowns with the man of my dreams. Here goes nothing!

Waking up that first morning as husband and wife was glorious. Life felt exactly as it should be. A whole new life was ahead of us, one that would be filled with many victories and celebrations, along with countless trials and challenges.

Real life—well, real life as a military spouse, didn't set in right away. Life was all peachy with David on leave and us on our honeymoon. We were free from distractions that come with being at home, back at work, and the Navy controlling all the things.

We wasted no time going to get our marriage certificate turned in, which allowed me to be added to David's insurance and issued an ID card. Maybe it's just me, but there's something that just makes you feel like you belong when you have your own ID! It meant now I could get on base without having to be escorted. I could now shop at the Navy Exchange (NEX) and the commissary, the military grocery store. Oh, happy day!

I remember thinking after we first got married that there needed to be some sort of "Welcome Spouse Kit" with all the things you needed to do and know when you marry your service member. The to-do list seemed long and neither of us really knew what we were doing. What did we need to take, and where, to get me added to insurance, to DEERS, etc.?

I told him one day I'd create such a kit, but here we are fifteen plus years in with no such kit or letter of instructions and I am probably just as useless now as I was then. Anyone else feel like that would have been helpful? Maybe it's just me and my need to have a list to check things off and be told *exactly* what I need to do. If you haven't figured out yet, you will quickly learn that the unknown and I don't do well.

I guess now would be no better time than ever to work on that list of things to do when you first get married. Flip to the back of the book to find my list of "helpful need-to-knows" as you begin your military life.

There is so much of the military life that is confusing, seems backward, and is hard to understand, even to this day. I decided when we first got married that I wanted to be involved. I wanted to understand and be in the know as much as I can. Not all spouses are, and it's definitely not a requirement.

For me, I was interested to know where David was working, what his job was, and all the things. In my opinion there's a bit of pride sharing with family and friends the work your spouse does who is serving our county. I know this isn't the case for everyone, and that's perfectly okay.

I dove into all the books: *Sea Legs: A Handbook for Navy Life and Service*[1], *Married to the Military*[2] by Meredith Leyva, and *The Complete Idiot's Guide to Life as a Military Spouse*[3]. I jumped on military forums and websites, and plugged into support groups like the FRG (Family Readiness Group). All those acronyms alone were enough to keep me busy for days.

I knew the day would come when I would have to navigate this life without him, while he was on the other side of the world. I knew I couldn't depend on communication to be fast or even regular, so I was determined to figure it out now and understand it, at least a little.

---

[1] U.S. Navy, *Sea Legs: A Handbook for Navy Life and Service, Rev. ed* (Washington, D.C.: Naval Services FamilyLine and CNIC, 1966).
[2] Meredith Leyva, *Married to the Military: A Survival Guide for Military Wives, Girlfriends, and Women in Uniform* (New York: Simon & Schuster, 2003).
[3] Lissa McGrath, *The Complete Idiot's Guide to Life as a Military Spouse.* (New York: Alpha Books, 2008).

THE BUILDUP

Each time deployment is less than a month away, no matter if it's the first time or your fifth, if you are newly married or now have a family, there is a tidal wave of emotions that start building. Our family has grown from being just David and I. We added two Great Danes, and now two kids. After three years of shore duty I forgot, or pushed aside, the debilitating emotions prior to deployment. But every deployment, the feelings resurfaced as David prepared to leave again, and now it isn't just me I have to worry about, but the kids too.

Suddenly the laundry, the dishes, the messy house, none of it mattered anymore. I wanted nothing more than to cling onto David and just pray that the reality of him leaving was only a bad dream.

I should know better than to be caught off guard by these last-minute changes in the military. I'm not sure whether the surprise and not much time to worry about it all is better or worse.

This, my friends, is one of the absolute hardest parts of military life!

I couldn't even come up with the words to tell my kids that

Daddy was leaving and not in a few months like we thought, but immediately.

As a military spouse and parent, there's nothing more heartbreaking than watching your kids crumble, hearing the news that Daddy must leave for an extended period of time, especially when they tell you daily how much they wish Daddy didn't have to go to work at all. I tasked David with giving the kids the news because I knew I would crumble. They handled it like the rock stars they are though.

I don't hold back the tears anymore. I want them to know it's okay that it's hard, that I struggle too. It's okay to cry and be sad, and together we will get through it.

We talk about it as much and as often as they want or need to. We will hold each other close, keep ourselves busy, and together make it to the end.

Deployment was coming. No matter how many times, or how hard I try to push it out of my head, to busy myself with the daily things and fun times with David, the days always get shorter and the tension grows stronger.

Wrapping my brain around the fact that half of an entire year, most likely more, is going to go by with David gone and not having the opportunity to see him feels suffocating and impossible.

When I let it get to me, which in those early years of military life happened often, I would tell myself that life is meant to be together, not apart. How can it be possible that his "work trip" is so long? Why does it have to be so long? How am I going to have enough strength to get through the days without him?

The feelings of anxiety and depression of him leaving didn't take the same form during every deployment. It was different and quite unpredictable. However, the ups and downs, the "I can do this" to "no I can't do this," to "how am I going to get through this long time apart?" leading up to your spouse leaving are real every time.

Heading into our first deployment we did all the things. My goal was to be intentional from the beginning to help us navigate future deployments as smoothly as possible. From the first deployment, you gain understanding of what to expect, you learn the things that help time pass and the things that don't, and you learn that you do indeed have the strength to survive a deployment.

Gearing up to deployment is stressful, there is tension and you want them just to hurry up and leave so they can get back home. David and I have done deployments on the boat and deployments to land bases. The boat, in my opinion is by far the most challenging. Communication is hit or miss depending on what the ship is doing and, some days, when life's been tough, you want nothing more than to hear their voice.

Perhaps you've heard of military members making a video of themselves reading a book so their children can see them and hear their voice while they are deployed. Well, we didn't have kids on that first deployment, but that didn't mean I didn't want a recording! I asked David to change his voicemail to a message for me. He so sweetly recorded a message that I could hear whenever I wanted. His phone would be turned off while on the ship, and he wouldn't have service in port. There was no way I could just pick up the phone to call him, so this was a solution to my problem. On the hard days, when I missed him terribly or just wanted to hear his voice, I would call his phone and listen to his sweet voice message for me.

Remember that covenant I shared with you in chapter two? It was written prior to that first deployment as another one of those things in hopes to set ourselves up well. Our covenant, while we don't necessarily review it each time he leaves or change answering machine recordings (technology has grown quite a bit since then!), I think he and I would agree that these things we first wrote down helped us build a solid starting foundation for our marriage.

During the first deployment or two, especially without kids, you do what you need to get through and only have yourself to worry about. As time went on, I thought deployments would get easier. They didn't. Looking back over those first few times David left, I didn't recognize what my feelings truly were. If you attend a pre-deployment briefing, they talk about these feelings and the cycles of grief. Yeah, yeah, I thought. That won't happen to me. I'll be fine!

But I wasn't fine.

I did a pretty good job pushing away all the feelings of deployment, and I didn't realize the toll each time David left took on me until yet another deployment was drawing close. This was deployment number four. Remember what happened the first time he left, the mess I was? Yes, that mess, the tears, the worry, all happened again and this time much, much worse.

Even before David left, I could barely function. Trying to process how I was feeling, I kept telling myself, "This is not my first rodeo! Why is this time so much harder? Why couldn't I just be back to normal?" In fact, the deployment before this one, David left while I was six months pregnant with Lucy, and even knowing she would be born while he was gone, such extreme feelings never surfaced.

With tears streaming down my face, I laid on the couch because getting up felt too hard. Not wanting to get up and feeling completely overwhelmed by sorrow, I laid pitifully on the couch while the kids played in front of me on the floor. I still couldn't believe I was feeling this way *this* time. I knew what to expect, how to stay busy, how to make it through, so *why* in the world was I struggling like I was? Perhaps not being able to accept my feelings only made it worse.

I couldn't wrap my head around why I felt so down when just last deployment I had a baby *without* my spouse. Nothing seemed harder and worse than that and yet here I was on the struggle bus *big* time.

My solution to the problem was to ignore my feelings and do my best to just keep moving. I told myself everything was fine, but I'm not sure I believed it.

My symptoms started to take the form of pregnancy, which of course only added to the worry. *I can't be pregnant again*, I thought. I laid down a lot, either having a difficult time getting out of bed in the morning, or putting activities in front of my kids, even the

TV, so I could just lay on the couch and sulk. Yes, that's what it was—sulking.

Again, I couldn't eat. Nothing sounded good and I felt nauseous thinking about or trying to eat. I just didn't feel like myself and it started to weigh on me more and more.

Finally, one day I looked at David with snot and salty tears running down my face, and told him it was time to seek professional help. How in the world was I going to keep us all alive through these upcoming months with me not being able to function?

I'm thankful my kids were so little at this point. Owen was just over three and Lucy about one and a half. They didn't realize what was going on and hopefully didn't feel the effects of the utter sadness I was feeling.

Please know this—these feelings before deployment are pretty normal, but it's so important to consult a professional. Be sure to check in with a doctor if you are feeling this way. There is no shame in seeking help!

Off to the doctor I went to have a discussion about what I was feeling. I needed a solution on how to move forward from here so I could carry on and take care of not only myself, but the two sweet babes God entrusted into my care. We also had two dogs who relied on me and only me for food, water, and to be let out.

I took a pregnancy test that day, because the symptoms were there, but it was negative. I breathed a sigh of relief with that confirmation. It wasn't that I wouldn't have been happy to have another baby. It was that life felt so overwhelming already, adding another responsibility to the picture only felt like a heavier weight.

During my appointment, the doctor looked me in the eyes and said, "Well, you have some depression."

Throughout this whole appointment I still didn't quite know how to put my feelings into words and honestly, it didn't even cross my mind that these feelings came with a diagnosis of *depression,* but perhaps I was scared about what it meant moving forward. Perhaps I was in denial. I mean, I was strong, independent, and had done this before. Maybe he was wrong? In the back of my mind though, I knew he wasn't. I sat there, trying to process this new information and questioned what was the next step towards healing.

While it was hard to hear, there's something about hearing a diagnosis that finally felt like I could take a breath because now I knew what was going on. It's always a relief to have answers, but at the same time my heart ached. How could I let myself get to this point? Why now? This isn't my first deployment. What am I supposed to do?

Time was running out before David had to leave. I needed to figure out how to pull myself together, but how? Even though I felt completely lost and lacking any motivation to get up, I knew I had to learn how to function, if anything, for Lucy and Owen's sake.

My doctor suggested I check in with the psychologist, and let me just say, counselors are an awesome outlet. I truly wish I was seeing one regularly now and am in the process of getting back to it. Being able to speak out loud what's weighing me down instead of trying to hide in the shadows seemed to take the power away from my worries. I felt lighter. Getting out of bed slowly became easier.

The psychologist asked me about my passions, what I like to do for me. He gave me some suggestions to find a project to work on, move my body, and pursue a passion. You got it! I can do those things. Well at least saying them out loud and thinking about them was easy. Knowing what to do and actually following through to *do* the work is a bit more challenging.

As I started to engage in the suggested activities, my joy started to return. I began to feel so much better.

Sometimes it's as simple as taking action to busy yourself with good things and sometimes it's not. Sometimes it takes medication and/or multiple counseling sessions. Please hear and believe me when I say there is no shame in that. Take care of you and ask for help when you need it.

In my experience, deployments don't get easier. They get more manageable, but there is also more fear and anxiety when you remember the hard experiences you've already faced and think about having to do it all over again, alone.

Besides dealing with my own emotions, tension between David and I starts to rise and tempers grow short. It's not necessarily anger, but more of a coping mechanism to deal with the fact that your spouse, who you love and married to spend life with, is going to be spending a significant time away from home and who knows how often you'll hear from them.

As the time approaches to say, "See you later," I find myself looking at the clock, counting how many hours we have left. If I let it, it will leave a pit in my stomach, an ache in my heart, and tears streaming all day long.

Time can feel like it goes so slow when you don't want it to. Then all the sudden it's flying, and there's nothing you can do to slow it down.

As much as I don't want David to go, I know once he does, the countdown begins until he is home. The tension right before a deployment is so real!

It's easy to let the sadness of David leaving take hold and dwell on what little time we have left, but instead, I choose to focus on spending the time we have together intentionally, focused on each other, knowing that this time apart is only temporary.

The days leading up to departure are not days to be sad but to be joyful and thankful for love we have for each other, a love that's so strong it hurts in the most beautiful and painful way.

• • •

When the dreaded day finally arrives, it feels far too quick. You wake up in the morning, if you even slept at all, and your heart aches from the moment you open your eyes. It never takes long for the tears to start flowing. I wish I could be one of those spouses that sits in the terminal with a smile on my face, holding all emotions together until I get in the privacy of my car, but I'm not. For me, it's a put the car in park, get out to switch places, unload his bags, a quick hug, kiss and, "See you soon," because I just can't bear the weight of him leaving any longer. It hurts and it hurts badly. I tell myself, the sooner he goes, the sooner we can count down to him coming back home.

Watching him walk away is brutal because I know it will be months before I get to hold him close again. It will be months before we can sit across the table to enjoy a meal together. It will be months before we can share the moments of life together again.

If you thought you would blink and the time would pass, you'd be wrong. If you thought, "Oh, it's only a few months it will go by fast," you're wrong. So much changes in the time they are gone and there's not much you can do but get up and do your best while letting the time pass. During the entire deployment, there is always that feeling of a hole in your heart that something valuable is missing.

The fear and struggle is real about whether they will love you for who you have become while they are gone. The mind and the enemy know how to play tricks on you when you are feeling down.

It's this buildup before deployment you don't hear about. It's the tension in your relationship created by trying to cope with the fact that your spouse is going to be gone for months on end and a return date home is just penciled in, never set in stone. It's what we so often don't like to share because it's hard, and quite possibly makes us look weak.

This buildup is the part those who have never experienced military life may not even realize goes on. Deployment is much more than the pretty homecoming pictures and the smiles on the day they return. It's easy to see homecoming and think that makes it all better, but that beautiful moment is nowhere near the whole story of deployment.

FOUR

THE GOOD, THE BAD, AND THE UGLY OF DEPLOYMENT

You tell yourself you'll be fine while he's gone. You even tell yourself you're looking forward to it because you can get all the things done you don't while he's home. The house will stay cleaner. There will be less laundry.

Then he leaves . . .

The house feels empty, lonely, and way too quiet at night. You stay up far too late getting absolutely nothing productive done. You're parenting alone and seem more on edge, or perhaps the kids feel it too and are acting out a little more than normal.

You realize getting the stuff done doesn't matter. You wish for the mess, the laundry, his presence around the house and his smell. Time can't pass fast enough! It's day one and already you take back ever thinking it would be fine with him gone.

Day One

The day finally comes you have to say, "See you later." Oh, the emotions on that day. The buildup from the last couple of weeks comes to a head. I'm not sure I can even put it all into words. Perhaps the one word for that dreaded day, at least in my life is *tears*, all the tears. I am a crier, so there will always be tears. I try to stay strong for the kids, but in my opinion, they need to see that I too am having a hard time with Daddy leaving.

It's one thing for me to have to say goodbye, but can I just say watching Owen and Lucy, my sweet littles, clenching Daddy's uniform with tears streaming down their faces telling him not to go is so much harder than me saying, "See you later." Goodness, I am in tears just writing this to you. See, I told you I was a crier!

Driving home from dropping David off for an unknown return date feels like a heavy weight has been placed on my shoulders and a hole placed inside me. That first day, making it through the entire deployment feels impossible and a load far too heavy to bear. You think of all the things he is going to miss, the holidays, birthdays, school activities and events. You think about when you will get to talk to him next, how often will you get to talk to him, and what happens when you really need him and can't talk to him at all.

On this first day, not much gets done. The kids and I lay on the couch, snuggling, talking, and crying about how much we already miss Daddy. We let it be okay to have those feelings.

Every time David leaves, I dream of the deployment wall I'm going to put up. You know, the ones that are Pinterest perfect. A whole wall is dedicated to a fancy map showing where Daddy is, a clock with the time it is in his world, pictures of Daddy and maybe even a countdown, if I'm that brave. This wall, even after all the deployments, has yet to become a reality. Just like a countdown until homecoming (hang tight for more on this one!), it's one of those things that sounds so great and yet never works out how it should.

Messages come flooding that first day, checking in on us to see how we are and usually those just make me cry harder. I'm one who would much rather have someone check in and say, "Hey! Thinking of you and praying for you all today," instead of "Hey! How's it going?" Because one, my answer will always be the same. It's hard and not at all fun, and isn't it obvious how I am doing? I mean my spouse just left for months on end. I am *not* jumping up with joy. Okay, maybe that's a bit harsh, but for me, having to talk about and relive the moments of saying "See you later," only make it worse as we try to pick ourselves back up and work to find a new normal while Daddy is gone.

It usually takes about a week or two for me to get into a routine. You become quite the independent soul, so much so that when he comes home, you forget that you don't have to carry in all the bags of groceries on your own, that he can help with bedtime and baths, and that he can keep the kids occupied.

As crazy as this may sound, doing the laundry the day David leaves or the day after when his last few items of clothing still lay at the bottom of the basket is so hard for me. Who knew you would miss washing the many items of his uniform that fill the laundry and have to be folded just right. There is just something about his smell that is comforting. I'd be lying if I said there weren't times I debated whether or not I'd wash these last few items. I have even asked him to leave a shirt behind and slept with it.

It's funny though, he and the kids usually have the most laundry and I find myself complaining about having to fold it all and put it away, but I'm reminded in this moment of the little things, like being thankful he's around to even have his laundry to do.

All the Other Days

Getting back into deployment mode after a good amount of time home, I have realized that deployments/homecomings have a bit of the same effect having a baby does. You forget some of those things that were hard and painful so you have the strength to do it again. Do you know what I'm talking about?

There are so many things from one deployment to the next that I forget. One of which is how mentally taxing and exhausting it is. I'm sleeping, but halfway through the day am totally burned out. There is no relief to come later in the day, no one to help put the kids to bed, do the dishes, cook the meals, clean up, take care of the dogs, and on and on. It's all on you!

$$\bullet \quad \bullet \quad \bullet$$

We are a people who like to give our opinions and, of course, for deployment everyone wanted to give advice (or perhaps they thought of it more as encouragement) on how to make it through.

That one piece of advice I remember so clearly, perhaps because I learned quickly it could actually cause more grief if I wasn't careful, was to stay busy. Just keep yourself busy and time will fly. He will be back before you know it. But wouldn't you know, of course, I would take that advice and take it to the extreme.

I'm sure you've heard before there is such thing as too much of a good thing. Let me assure you it is most definitely true with busyness too.

During the first deployment, I was going to school, planning a wedding, volunteering weekly to tutor for an afterschool program, in a small group, working as a nanny part time, and more. I was on overload and it was just a matter of time before I crumbled.

When your spouse leaves for a period of time, it is important to stay busy so you aren't just sitting and feeling sad, watching the time tick by slowly—but there is a balance to how busy you are.

Another lesson I learned early on, was *do not* count down the days until your spouse or significant other will return. For one, the date is constantly changing and two, the days drag on and on and on. Oh, and the worst part—the time I learned this was just a workup, meaning it was a shorter time gone in preparation for the long deployment.

This first time he left, I thought it would be such a great idea to get crafty and make a countdown chain counting down each day of his month-long trip. Making the chain went great, the evening every day after that, not so much! I dreaded having to take on a full day before being able to count another day down.

I often hear spouses say that sleeping while their other half is gone is so hard. Not for me, except for that one time I made that countdown chain.

Each evening I would take another ring off the chain. Hooray, another day closer but instead of excitement about another day down, the way it felt to me was, "Oh great! now I have a whole new day to face before I can count another day closer to wrapping my arms around him." I should have stopped after the first few days when I realized my feelings overwhelmed me, but I didn't. Maybe I had hope one of those evenings I would finally feel better.

I thought ahead to the deployment, how long the chain would have to be, and how awful I would feel every evening. It was after that first and only time I vowed never to use a countdown chain, except as the final countdown (ten days or less) when waiting to hug my sailor again.

• • •

In the heart of deployment, the days seem to go forever, like the light at the end of the tunnel will never come.

Getting through the days means interacting with others who are often curious, or possibly just trying to create small talk and feel the need to ask how long your spouse has been deployed, or how much longer they will be gone. Now let me warn you, unless this person has experienced deployment, their response just might not be what you want to hear.

"Oh, three months! That's not too long!" As you pick your jaw up off the floor at the audacity to say such a thing, especially when your heart is feeling more emotional than ever, you try to think of a kind response.

Perhaps you respond with something along the lines of, "Well, sure, I suppose it's not as long as some other deployments, but he's still gone. Gone is gone and in this moment it's hard."

Sometimes those with the best intentions just don't quite understand and they probably never will unless they can experience it themselves.

Have you ever been asked the question, "How do you do it?" The answer, in my opinion, is simple. You just do. You enter a space of straight-up survival mode. What other choice do you have? I've learned you can sit and dwell in the pain and misery of it all or get up and do your best to take on each day with a smile.

Sometimes the reality of how long your spouse has been gone doesn't hit until he's back home and you're recalling recent memories. "Hey babe, do you remember when we went to do [insert activity]?" He looks at you with a confused expression. "I wasn't here, remember?" My memory becomes a blur and I can no longer remember what he was here for or what he wasn't.

The Deployment Curse

Each day of deployment is an adventure, especially with what military spouses like to call the deployment curse. Have you heard of it? It hit hard right away for me right at the beginning. The deployment curse is when all the things that could go wrong, things you want or need your spouse for, always seem to wait so patiently to happen until your spouse is not there to help you. Because they are on the other side of the world. In a different time zone. Sleeping.

In these moments, even though you want nothing more than to crumble to the ground, curl up in a ball, and cry, you realize you are so much stronger than you ever thought. You take a deep breath, make the phone call and get whatever done that needs to be done to fix what happened. Some of the things that happen, you just can't make up!

You might be wondering how often these moments happen during deployment. Well, probably a lot more than I could even count. There are countless times I pick up my phone to call David while he is deployed, only to start dialing and realize that I can call (as long as he's not on the ship), but his phone will ring to voicemail, and it will be hours before I can talk to him. He's not here to help me fix it. It's funny how no matter how long he's gone, it's still automatic to try to call him first.

Our first deployment started off swimmingly. It was the day after David left—that first day the deployment curse hit.

I remember thinking, "Come on, couldn't we have at least waited a few months, or even weeks?" The answer was, of course, nope! The deployment curse is unpredictable, but practically a guarantee.

Let me set the scene for you. I stopped by our indoor storage unit to grab something or drop something off. What it was, I have no idea anymore. What happened while I was there took over the memory of the visit itself.

You're probably wondering why we even had a storage unit. At this point, we were engaged and had been gifted some incredible furniture for our first place once we got married. We had to find a place to store it all until that time came. It was something way too good to pass up. Side note . . . nothing makes me realize how long we've been married than looking at some of our furniture and realizing we've had it since the beginning. Some of that furniture we stored is still around!

The storage place was all indoor and had an elevator. Great, right? Our stuff would be dry and warm, but one thing we failed to pay attention to was the fact that navigating these indoor hallways was hard and I would have to get on and off an elevator. Let me tell you one of my absolute greatest fears . . . getting stuck in an elevator! It was always one of those fears I could talk myself out of as irrational, until that day.

I stepped into the elevator and pressed the number to get to the second floor. The elevator went up but abruptly stopped within just a few short seconds. I knew surely I hadn't made it to the second floor and my fear was realized when I stood there waiting for the doors to open and they did not. Panic set in, my heart began to race, and I frantically searched around the elevator for what to do next. I needed out, and fast!

It took everything within me not to crumble into a ball of tears right then. Just being at the storage unit reminded me that I just said, "See you later," for who knows how long and now my worst nightmare of being stuck in an elevator had just come true. Only on a deployment would this happen!

I managed to pull myself together, found the emergency call button, and as calmly as I could, talked to the operator on the other end. They let me know that someone would soon be on the way to get me out.

The minutes felt long as I waited for them to come. I had no cell service, so I couldn't call anyone, which I suppose is a good thing because chances are if someone on the other end was able to answer, the tears would have immediately started flowing.

When those doors opened, it was like a huge sigh of relief and I felt like I could finally breathe again. I can't tell you if I was brave enough to get back on the elevator and do what I had planned to do that day or not. I just remember getting off and never wanting to go back there again, or at least not alone. It was only day one, and it already felt so hard. Nothing like kicking this whole military life thing off with a bang!

Another one of these moments for the books . . .

Owen (who was probably two years old at the time), Lucy (less than one year old), and I pulled into the garage after running errands. Owen loved to play with my keys. I had a push start ignition, so I would let Owen hold them while I was driving. It was no big deal, until the one day it was, but you probably already knew that, didn't you?

I got out of the car and the second, not two or three seconds, but immediately after, he pushed the *lock* button from inside the car. He was oblivious about what he had just done. Lucy was fast asleep and none the wiser, thankfully. But, me, I was in complete panic mode. I walked over to Owen's side, and as calm as a completely panicked mom can do, tried to direct him how to unlock the car. Wouldn't you know that every time he pushed a button it was the *lock* button, over and over and over! That panic I felt, and didn't know it could get worse, escalated to the point of Owen starting to feel my panic. Tears started rolling, both his and mine. Surely it couldn't get worse, unless, of course, he dropped the keys, couldn't unbuckle to get out of his seat, and finally push the unlock. Oh yes, it happened!

Who do you call in that moment when you're so upset, can't think straight to solve your problem, and can't get your kids out of the car? Mom, of course! Thankfully, I had my phone. Somehow, I had the wherewithal to keep that with me. Phew!

With tears streaming down my face, and in between sobs, I told my mom what happened and that I was at a loss as to what to do. Mom did what she always does best. She calmed me down and gave me some advice, which was to call a locksmith. Sometimes we are blinded from the most obvious answer in the moment of complete panic.

Good news, the locksmith I called could come in only twenty minutes. That, my friends, felt like the longest twenty minutes *ever*, but I started to breathe a little more. Owen, not so much. He was still in the car all worked up, knowing he was stuck.

Having time to wait for the locksmith allowed a funny thing to happen. I had time to think, and I started to get mad. Was it warranted? Nope, but it happened. I thought, why in the world did David need his keys when he was over there across the globe and the car was here? I also was calm enough to remember that I did indeed have a phone number to get a hold of David.

So, I called David, praying he would hear it (he's a very heavy sleeper) and answer. He did! I was relieved, but then immediately questioned him about his keys and then angrily blamed him. Like it's his fault this thing happened in the first place, right?

His response to the whole situation was, "Okay, what do you want me to do?" This of course just made me more upset, even though I knew he couldn't help. I knew there was nothing he could do. I just needed, or maybe wanted, to hear his voice and vent. My response to him wasn't calm or fair to him on the other side of the world, but nonetheless, I said, "I know you can't do anything. I just wanted you to know!"

Shortly after getting off the phone with David, the locksmith arrived. After looking over my car, a Volkswagen, he told me he might actually have to break my car window, because it had tamper-proof windows. As if I thought it couldn't get worse!

Thankfully, he didn't break the window, and he was able to unlock the door and set my kids free. Lucy at this point still had not woken up.

The lesson from it all—well, actually there were two. First, David doesn't need to take all his keys with him, and no longer does. Second, don't let your baby who *loves* to push buttons, but doesn't know which is which, play with your keys in the car.

• • •

It might seem so far that deployment is awful. While I wouldn't say it's good or something I look forward to, great blessings and joy can come from deployment. Getting through a deployment feeling joyful at the end requires gratitude along the way. Gratitude can be found in each day and in every circumstance. Sometimes you have to look a little bit harder to find it, but it's there.

One of my favorite things about deployment is the chance to get to know other military spouses. You are surrounded by a community that knows how you feel, and may even be going through what you're going through. I encourage you, if you are getting ready for a deployment or will have the duty of navigating through one sometime in the future, find a buddy whose spouse is also gone to walk on the journey with you.

For me, this looked like having a friend over every other week for dinner. Earlier, I mentioned how counting down the days of deployment can have the feeling of time slowing down. That still holds true, but if you put something on your schedule to look forward to every two weeks, like a dinner night with a friend, enough time passes to allow you to feel like a good chunk has passed since the last time you were together. This means you are that much farther though deployment and can celebrate another two weeks down!

Taking turns, we would cook a meal to share together. The evening was spent in great conversation, quite possibly even complaining some about how the deployment is going, and just being a support for one another.

I'm not sure I would say this makes deployment worth it, but I definitely would not take back the time I had with my dear friend, Bethany. Over the course of two deployments our friendship grew, we found great strength in one another, and were able to celebrate the victories and joys of deployment together.

Not everyone is going to understand what you are going through during deployment, and that's okay. We can't expect people to, especially if they have never experienced it.

The deployments I fared the best, with the most strength, emotional stability, and joy, were the ones that I had other women on the journey with me. Whether I was plugged into the Family Readiness Group (FRG) or had regularly scheduled dates with friends, these things were so helpful, dare I even say necessary, in surviving during deployment.

Just like anything else in life, we aren't meant to do it alone. Find those people you can do deployment with. If that friend is only with you during that season for whatever reason, embrace having them by your side, and know they were placed in that season for a purpose.

Deployment Baby

I always tell people I'd not wish having a baby without your spouse on my worst enemy, and it's the truth. It's hard to do life alone as it is, but having a baby alone makes you even more Wonder Woman in my book than you already are as a military spouse.

I remember standing at my first FRG meeting near a gal who had a five-week-old baby and her husband had just deployed. I looked at her and thought, "I so want David to be present and not miss the birth of our babies." I selfishly worried about me and at the same time my heart broke for her as she went at this parenting thing alone with her first newborn.

This woman became one of my most absolute dear friends and has encouraged me in so many ways. I'm so blessed to call her friend still today! Oh, and in case you're wondering, that deployment with her five-week-old baby, she navigated it like a rock star!

That word, *never,* was what I'd said about having a baby without David. Funny how God has a sense of humor, and it happened despite my longing for it not to. We both had to trust in God's timing. The Lord no doubt helped me navigate that time without David. There are days I still wonder how the kids and I survived. Now I get to share my story and use it to encourage others walking through this same experience. Life in the military is unpredictable and births while their daddy is away happen way more than you'd hope.

Let's be real, planning anything while in the throes of military life is hard. Add planning a baby to that, which is hard in and of itself. The Navy is awesome (said with the utmost sarcasm) at changing their plans last minute and a million times over, so even though you planned, it doesn't work out in your favor.

I remember the day I found out I was pregnant with Lucy. After getting over the shock of being pregnant, which felt like so soon after having Owen, my mind went immediately to the panic of whether David would be home or not. Deployment was on the horizon. I did the math and realized that David would be deployed—on the other side of the world—and miss the birth of our second baby. I bet you can guess what happened next. Tears, and lots of them. The tears were not at all that we didn't want another baby, because we did. It was just hard to grasp the fact that what I *never* wanted to happen was now indeed going to happen.

I'm a firm believer that everything happens for a reason and she is no mistake, but as I sat there thinking about her not having her Daddy to hold her on day one, I couldn't help but sob. Tears streamed down my face, not because she would know he wasn't there, but because I would. Because there wouldn't be any pictures of him in the hospital holding her. Because she wouldn't have those first few months of her life to start bonding with him. Because I would be alone raising two kids under two. Just the thought of it was exhausting!

Pulling myself together, I realized I would have to break the news to David when he got home from work that day. I knew it would be just as hard for him as it was me, if not harder. It's a moment you want to be so joyous about but knowing you will be doing it apart from each other felt absolutely crushing.

As he sat on the couch that afternoon, I remember going to sit next to him and give him the news. I can't even remember how I told him, but I remember his response so clearly. Anger! Like my tears, his anger wasn't because we were having another baby. It was anger from frustration, because he also quickly figured out that he would not be home for the birth, and not likely until months after her birth.

Only rarely is a military member sent home for a birth when you're in the line of duty and deployed overseas. We both knew that and had to come to terms with it, but was it easy? No way!

As delivery drew closer, I went into labor. Not only was my husband not going to be there for Lucy's birth, but I feared that my parents wouldn't either. They were living on the other side of the country. Everyone felt so far away. I laid in the hospital bed that first time in labor, and just cried out of loneliness. It wouldn't be until the third time in the hospital before Lucy decided to make her grand entrance into the world.

This is a common theme in the military, being without any family close by. Thankfully, even though my family was far away at this point, I wasn't alone. I had the incredible support of my military family. They made sure Owen was taken care of and that I had everything I needed.

Lucy decided it wasn't time for her arrival yet that first hospital visit, so back home we went. Thankfully, my parents arrived before she did. While it wasn't the same as having David there, I was so relieved. Moms always make things better, wouldn't you agree?

Early on a Friday morning, I woke up to Owen crying. I climbed out of bed to check on him and as I got to my feet, contractions came what felt like out of nowhere, and hard!

I went to wake up my mom and told her it was go time. Because I had been to the hospital twice before, my mom thought she had time to do some stretches and we'd leave in a little bit. That wasn't the case this go around. Walking was literally a pain. I waddled my way to my bathroom where my hospital bag was, grabbed it, and hurried back to get my mom. I'm not sure she realized until that moment that time was of the essence and we needed to get moving, now!

On the ride to the hospital, Mom asked if she would need to show identification (ID) to get through the Navy base gate. I assured her it would be fine because I would be able to hand them mine, but it wasn't that easy.

Pulling up to the gate right around 4:00 am, I did my best to reach over and hand the guard on duty my ID. At that moment I was at the height of a contraction and was doing my best to reach as far as I could but couldn't quite reach out the window. In a stern voice, he said, "Ma'am, I can't reach into your vehicle to get your ID." My mom took my ID from me and handed it out the window. Then he said, "I need to see your ID also, ma'am." Fumbling through her purse, she scrambled to find her ID. Finally, it dawned on the guard that there was something a little off. He looked into the car again, and I'm assuming saw me in pain or perhaps on the edge of tears, and asked, "Is everything okay?"

"No! I am in labor!" I'm pretty sure my tone was not the friendliest. I mean why else would a pregnant woman be driving through the gate at some ridiculous hour in the early morning? The guard panicked and quickly waved us on.

The drive to the hospital felt forever long, but in reality, was only just a few minutes. The contractions kept coming and they weren't slowing down. As we pulled into the parking lot, I realized the daunting walk I would have to make down to Labor and Delivery. Most days the doors don't feel too far away, or a nice little walk is a good thing, but not this day. Labor and Delivery was at the opposite end of the hospital. Because of the early hour, the door closest was locked. I'm not sure how to explain walking in that morning other than I felt like I was hunched over like an old lady with a stick up my rear.

David was on the phone checking in because I sent him an urgent message that our sweet Lucy, who was definitely running the show and controlling the timing, was surely coming today.

Out of breath and ready to get this baby out, I made it to check in at Labor and Delivery. I leaned on the counter because standing without support wasn't going to happen at the rate and intensity of those contractions. I remember looking at the nurse that early morning and letting her know, "She's coming!" They didn't believe me.

The nurse ushered me into a room. Thankfully it was only across the hall. Changing out of my clothes and into the gown was incredibly challenging with the pain from the contractions. It wasn't more than a few minutes of laying in the bed, after being checked and already dilated to six centimeters, that my water broke.

Everything happened so fast. I was in shock that my water broke but knew the result of that happening. My contractions, already intense, were going to intensify even more. I couldn't hold back the tears. Through the tears, I told my mom to go and grab the nurse.

Having Owen, my first, I wanted to do all things natural. This go around, I was okay having an epidural, so I asked for the anesthesiologist, but at four something in the morning they had to be called in and there was no time for that.

I don't remember much of any conversation from the nurse that morning, other than the constant reminder to, "blow out the candles." That seemed impossible. My body had a mission and it was to out this baby. I wanted to scream at the nurse to let her know that I was doing all I could to just breathe!

White knuckled and clenching the side of the bed, my mom stood beside me with my phone in hand and David on FaceTime. He was "there," I guess you could say. This was the best we could do with him thousands of miles away. Thank goodness for internet service that morning that most days was sketchy at best. He didn't miss a minute of her birth.

I could tell the nurse was starting to panic. My pain was high and I could feel Lucy coming down. In desperation, I asked, "What are we waiting for?"

"The doctor!" she responded.

Finally, the doctor walked in, they rolled me on my back, and out came Lucy. No pushes required. My physical relief was instant. I laid there and just tried to breathe. When I finally realized I just had a baby, I asked to cut the umbilical cord since David wasn't there.

The doctor replied, "Um, I already did." If I were with it, I may have been upset because I had asked before delivering to do it, but being out of it, I simply responded, "okay."

What I didn't know was that when Lucy was born, she was a bit blue because her cord wrapped around her neck twice. The cord was cut so she could breathe and for that I am so thankful. So many things could have gone wrong, and yet I felt completely covered and wrapped in the protection of the Lord.

It felt surreal lying in bed holding my newborn while David was on the other side of the ocean. One of the things I never expected to happen in this military life happened and there was nothing I could do but accept it and deal with it the best I could.

A corpsman came in to ask a few questions and fill out paperwork. I don't remember any of the questions he asked but one, "Was Dad present?" Meaning was Dad there for the birth. I laughed and said, "Well, he was on FaceTime." The corpsman replied as he circled the answer on his sheet, "Yes!" No, no he was not! FaceTime did not count because he was not here to hold his beautiful and precious newborn and wouldn't be able to for another three months or so.

Lucy's birth and the things that followed her arrival all happened in a span of less than thirty minutes. While I so wish David was there that day to be holding my hand in the height of my contractions and getting to hold our sweet newborn that first day of her life, I am so thankful for technology and him still being able to be a part and to witness her birth. I will never have pictures of David holding Lucy in the hospital, which is hard for me, but Lucy doesn't know the difference.

Because everything happened so fast, I was not able to get the medication I needed in my body before Lucy was delivered, so we had at least 48 hours to spend in the hospital and be under watch. That was the loneliest hospital stay ever. Friends and family came and went throughout the day, but the moments it was just Lucy and I felt far too quiet. I wanted nothing more than to have David beside me staring lovingly into the sweet eyes of our newborn and keeping me company during the moments the quiet threatened to overtake me. No hospital stay is the same without your spouse. Lucy and I had a lot of time to bond, just me and her. Perhaps that's why she is such a momma's girl now.

I'm forever thankful God surrounded me with nurses and doctors I knew during Lucy's birth, giving me some sense of calm and peace with all the change that was happening.

In the midst of the excitement of Lucy's birth, Owen, just under two years old, was not sure what was going on. Mommy was in the hospital, Daddy was gone, and he was about to meet a new member of the family.

I knew the change would be hard for him, especially under the circumstances. Filled with excitement when he came to meet his sister, my bubble was quickly burst when he walked into the room, wanted nothing to do with her or me. In fact, he spit at me.

I honestly don't remember my response but can only imagine that my heart sank and my eyes welled with tears I tried to hold back. I wanted to be strong for Owen. I wanted him to know that he was still just as dearly and deeply loved as before.

Those first two weeks of Lucy's life were incredibly hard. Owen made sure to let me know how much he opposed having a new sibling. He knew just when I sat down to nurse and was preoccupied, for these were the times he climbed the counters and did all the things he knew he wasn't supposed to. Oh, if only David had been home to help.

I did the only thing I knew how to do, and that was question if I was doing this whole mother thing right. Maybe we shouldn't have had another baby, but clearly I couldn't change that.

The rest of that deployment was a blur as we tried to navigate the new changes at home and stay afloat with David still gone.

What an amazing day homecoming was this go around! It always is but that day would be special because Lucy got to meet David for the first time and the pictures show just how priceless that memory is. It's a day I'll never forget.

I prayed every day that Owen would begin to love his sister. Thankfully, that day came. The two of them now have the most special bond, and I couldn't be more thankful it all worked out in the end.

• • •

Extension . . . the one word while your spouse is deployed that you never want to hear, yet can almost count on hearing.

With homecoming drawing closer, you are longing to hear the actual date of arrival back home. You know better than to start planning anything until you have a hard date. Even when a date is "final," you know to keep your plans flexible because all too often the Navy changes their plans last minute.

A short time into that first deployment, I experienced the feelings attached with *extension*. Word came down from the chain of command that there was a delay for one reason or another. It's so easy to get upset and be mad, but I've learned that all this does is create a negative mindset, making time feel like it goes by that much slower. Is it frustrating? Oh, yes! Does it affect plans you were hoping to pan out? Most likely!

What if, though, you could find something positive about the extension and hold on to that while you wait? Maybe you will have more time to get the house in order just how you want it. Perhaps now you can go and find that perfect homecoming outfit you originally thought you didn't have time for. Or maybe it's as simple as reminding yourself that your reunion will be that much sweeter.

• • •

Before homecoming happens, a brief (meeting) is held to remind spouses of what to expect when our sailor comes home. I will never forget the first brief I went to and the diagram drawn on the whiteboard that day. It looked like this . . .

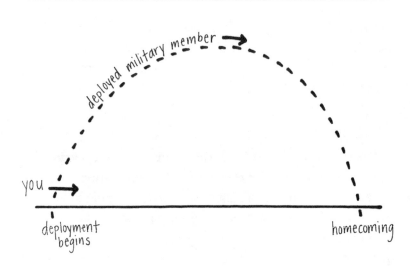

The picture and description are so simple and yet so powerful. You, the ones holding down the home front, are the straight line. You experienced life all along the way. The sailor is the rainbow line or the arc. You were doing life together at the start and then he did a little hop, skip, and a jump missing all the in between and now is jumping back into life right where you are after missing so much of life that happened along the way. Life will look and feel different than it did when he left. It is a transition that requires time to adjust.

Homecoming almost makes the entire deployment worth it. I always tell myself that those first few minutes you reunite with your loved one. It's like the honeymoon period all over again. You look at your spouse in the same way you did when you were still dating or newly married. You know that feeling, right? It is the feeling of absolute love where nothing else in the world matters. It's a feeling that seems to wear off over the years of marriage.

After many long days, weeks, and months, the day you've been waiting for and counting down to has finally arrived. All the feelings seem to rush over you. The excitement, nerves, and butterflies probably started yesterday as you prepared those last-minute details to make the day just right.

As soon as you hang the homecoming banner welcoming them home, it finally starts to feel real.

You want the house to be perfectly clean, no dirt or dust left behind, like they'd even notice the smallest speck. Chances are the cleanliness of the house is the last thing on their mind. But still, you feel the pressure to clean. You know that over the course of deployment you may have let some of the things you usually kept up with slide, and for good reason. Doing life alone while your spouse is deployed means all the extra duties become yours.

Before heading to bed that night, you lay out your clothes and the kids' clothes. You double check with the photographer and make sure they are up to date with the latest time information. You know as well as I do that this time can change what feels like fifty times and never is quite right. You show up an hour early just in case they get in early.

Standing in the hangar, there are smiles and laughter in anticipation of the moment the plane comes into view. You can't stand still and find yourself pacing back and forth across the hangar. You may have just endured six plus months of separation, but this last hour can feel like eternity.

You start to see people pointing out the hangar doors, so you look and see it too. The plane with your sailor on it is finally in sight. They really are home! I never fully believe they will actually be back when they are say until I see them. Too many changes and delays leave me a bit skeptical.

As the plane taxis, excitement builds. The kids keep asking where Daddy is. It's like a long car trip and constantly being asked, "Are we there yet? Are we there yet?" but instead it's, "Is Daddy here yet? Is Daddy here yet? When is he going to be here?"

Do you know how slow a plane taxis? *Slow!* Do you know how long it takes for that door to open? *Forever!* I always wonder what all the military members sitting on the plane are thinking when they can see their family members waiting at the edge of the hangar. Are they just as antsy to get off the plane as we are waiting for them?

Finally, a sea of people in their camouflage uniforms files off the plane. You have no idea, most likely, where in the plane your sailor is so you find yourself constantly scanning the crowd of everyone who looks the same to find that familiar face.

As you stand at the end of the hangar behind the line you're not supposed to cross, at least yet, you wait and hesitate on whether you can step out of the hangar to be in the arms of your sailor again.

Those around you encourage you, "Go!" You are told to walk, but at this point, all bets are off! You've spotted your sailor and now it's all a matter of holding back the tears of joy.

Reaching your sailor, he bends down and the kids jump into his arms, because chances are they beat you to Daddy. There is nothing sweeter than wrapping your arms around your spouse again for the first time in months. You hold on, not wanting to let go. The only words you can get out are "I love you!" You hug and kiss, making up for all the lost time.

Once again you feel whole. In that moment, everyone around you disappears and it's just you and your family.

You walk back to the hangar, hand in hand, maybe grabbing some food that was brought to snack on, even though food is the last thing on your mind. All you want to do is be back home together as a family, snuggling up on the couch and catching up on all the time that was lost.

Finally in the car, you're headed home, with your sailor behind the wheel. Hopefully he remembers how to drive after six plus months. Maybe it's just me, but it's such a great feeling when I don't have to be the sole driver anymore. Being together as a family has never felt so good.

Homecoming day is just the start of getting reacquainted and used to being a family unit again. I wish I could tell you they come home and life goes back to being what it was before they left, but that wouldn't be the truth.

There is a good amount of anxiety and stress that accompanies the joy and excitement. If you're anything like me, you play all the what-ifs in your mind. Will he still love me? Have I changed over the last six months? Has he changed over the last six months? How will the kids react? The questions can go on and on. This is just a little peek into my brain, as the transition to being whole again starts. It's not as easy as it might seem or those homecoming pictures make it look. There is always a readjustment period.

Reintegration with your spouse is exciting but it doesn't change the fact that things have changed while your spouse was gone. There can be a little bit of tension at first and sometimes a few bumps in the road as you get used to each other again. Your spouse is relearning and reestablishing their parenting role, and role at home. You likely have new routines, new activities, and maybe some discipline practices changed. It takes time to get adjusted, and that's okay. Communication during this time is key as you work through it all. For those outside the military, know that with any homecoming there is so much more behind the homecoming pictures filled with smiles celebrating that day you welcome them home and hug them again for the first time. Adding your spouse back in is not always the easiest and most joyous time at first. Knowing it is an adjustment and expecting there to be some ups and downs can help you navigate the transition with much more grace and intention.

FIVE

MOVING DAY

The anticipation for a move begins *far* before the day you drive away. Why, you might ask? Because it involves change and change is always hard, or at least it is for me anyway. It always seems that just as you get comfortable at your duty station, when all the pictures are finally hung in their places, and the last of the boxes are emptied and recycled, the kids comfortable with their friends and you with yours, that's when it's time to move.

A year out from moving and the excitement builds about the possibility of new adventure! The excitement at this point outweighs any sadness that might come with a move. Where you could go seems endless and you are completely hopeful that you will get a *choice* in where the military sends you next.

At first, the thought of living in a new location feels like a fun, new adventure. Maybe you haven't loved your current duty station. This makes orders for two, three, or four years a good thing. You can't wait for something new that has to be better than here. This is a funny thing, though you usually don't realize until later. The grass isn't always greener elsewhere and dare I say you miss more than you thought you ever would about the duty station you couldn't wait to leave.

Up until now, you are still holding on to the hope of a new, fabulous place to live. You dream about the "perfect" duty station, sure that it actually exists. All these feelings are still alive because orders still have not been released. You haven't looked at the list to see what's really there and available.

Reality hits the moment the order windows opens and closes. Where are all the options of the *fun* and *perfect* places we could go? It almost seems like the list is lying. This can't be real, but it is and with little to no options, your hope quickly fades. That excitement you once had when the process first started of moving to a new place and new adventure turns into worry and disappointment. The unknown that once left you full of hope leaves you feeling far from that and much more anxious.

Maybe I'm not like others, and some of you *love* the excitement, the unknown, and the ups and downs of the order process.

Most days, I am able to keep myself busy and focused on the present to push the unknown of orders, the frustration, and anxiety back and remind myself that God has the most perfect plan. I remind myself that this is where my hope should be, but then are the days it gets the best of me because I'm human and worry causes me to lose sight of Him.

It's all the what-ifs. What if we can't find housing? If you're not familiar with military housing, the wait lists can be long and you aren't guaranteed a house when you get to your new duty station. It's hard to feel calm about not knowing if you will have a place to live when you arrive in this new place you are to call home. What if Elsie (the dog) struggles with the change? What if the kids are miserable? What if we don't have time to get everything together? What if . . .

This is the reality of life right now as I write and I'm definitely in the valley of the days getting the best of me. You'd think by now, fourteen years in the military, I'd know this is normal and would be used to it. But even as a seasoned spouse, I struggle, and dare I say, I struggle more than early on in our military career. I guess each time I hope it will be different and low and behold, it's the same! Ha! Joke is on me.

Even in the hard moments of fear in the unknown, God gently taps me to remind me it's all okay, that it will all work out. He never promised life would be easy, that there wouldn't be battles or pain, but He did promise it will all work together for good and that He has only the best plan for my family and me when I surrender and let Him guide me.

This verse continues to speak life over me and perhaps it's what you need now too, whether you are in the process of a move or life just seems to keep throwing challenges your way.

"So let us come *boldly* to the throne of our gracious God. There we will receive his *mercy*, and we will find *grace* to *help* us when we need it most" (Hebrews 4:16, NLT, emphasis mine).

• • •

The week has come! It's our third, and *final*, window of picks and far too close to becoming "needs of the Navy," a place we've never been in our career of almost fourteen years and let me tell you, I'm not a fan. It feels a bit like do or die. It's much easier to feel like we are awaiting our *fate*, but perhaps I need a different perspective and should rather think of it as an incredible opportunity and adventure, a little change in mindset. I'd be lying though if I said the three words "needs of the Navy" didn't scare me at all. For those unfamiliar with the term, essentially it means the Navy will place us wherever they need us and our say in the matter is zero.

It never feels as bad to move somewhere, even when it's not where you wanted to go, when you had a little bit of a say, right? It's a "choice" like parents give their children. You can have a banana or an apple, which one do you want? Except in this choice I'm on the side making the choice instead of giving the options and I know better to believe that the choice is truly mine.

You'd think the longer you've been in and the higher up you go you've earned your right to get to choose where you want to go . . . wrong! It becomes much more slim pickings, at least for us, the farther we go in this journey.

I've done my best to put it all out of my mind but it seems to always be there. I think, "If only I knew where we were going, I'd feel better," but will I? Perhaps there's a reason it's taking some time. The good news is that God has perfect timing, so I have no doubt if I can let go of what I'm trying to control (even though I am not really even in control, I just tell myself I am), and give it to God, I will be at more peace.

And wouldn't you know God shows up in the midst of it all? He's really been there all along; I was just doing what I do best and trying to control the situation. During my quiet time and devotions, I am often reminded that I can fully trust God with the way things happen, which means not trying to predict or control outcomes of this Navy life and the moves that come along with it. Psalm 37: 4–5 (NLT) says, "Take delight in the LORD, and he will give you your heart's desires. Commit everything you do to the LORD. Trust him, and he will help you."

Thank goodness for summer and the activities we had going on. The busyness kept my mind occupied more often than not, almost to the point that getting some kind of news snuck up on me.

Of course, timing would have it that I was on a trip with my best girlfriends, but honestly, there's no one else I'd rather have around me to hug me and love on me when the news came and the Lord knew I needed them.

My phone lay right in front of me on the table we were gathered around as I waited anxiously for the call from David with news. Every minute, maybe even less, I was checking my phone to make sure I didn't miss his call. I was physically present as we stood around the table chatting, but my mind wasn't.

Suddenly my phone on the table started to buzz. It was David. My heart started to race. Everything in that moment stopped as I picked up and listened to David. All eyes were on me as my friends waited to hear too.

I could feel my eyes welling up with tears and my voice getting shaky, trying to hold it together while talking to David. Our conversation was brief, and when I hung up, I fell apart!

"You guys!" I cried, not just a little but a big ugly cry in front of all the girls.

It took a good amount of time to process it all and I'd be lying if that first day of hearing the news was the only day that brought me to tears about it. Before we knew this would be the outcome, I told David if a certain duty station came up, the one where we literally just four months prior sold our house after a rough go with renters, then it would take some major heart work to feel good about it. Well here we are. Insert heart work classes 101 because I was going to need them!

You should know, I was bitter and angry for weeks leaving Whidbey, our previous tour, because it was home, it was comfortable, and it was close to family. We had orders to stay and the Navy pulled them last minute, leaving us no option but to go where we were told. Here I was again, now crying that we are going back, and those tears were not happy tears. Shocker, I know!

It's not that I didn't want to go back, it's not that I didn't have so many people I love there and was excited to see, it wasn't that I didn't want to be close to family, because I did. I wanted all those things, but at the same time I had my heart wrapped up and excited about change and adventure somewhere else. My heart, and I think David's too, longed for Florida.

I thought for sure God was prepping my heart for somewhere other than home because for once in my life, I felt a desire for adventure somewhere totally new and for me this was huge! I love to live in my comfort zone, so to feel this longing, strength, and even confidence about a brand-new place all the way across the country felt like a sign that it was going to happen. Perhaps God, who sees all, knew even though I felt ready, I really wasn't ready yet. Perhaps

He was seeing if I'd answer the call to go somewhere other than back home.

Whatever it is, God has a plan for us and I know that it is far better than mine. It's a plan to bless, grow, and change us as a family. In the moment it's hard, really hard, and there is no sugar coating it. We will continue on, one day at a time, not worrying about the next because each day has its own troubles.

As we were processing the news of where we were headed, it still, in my opinion, wasn't time to start setting things in motion for the move. This was just *selection* of orders. We were penciled in, which in the military world doesn't mean a whole lot. Until orders were final, I didn't want to let my guard down that Whidbey was for sure. Things have changed on us in the past after this point, so I felt like, while there were some answers, we were still hanging in the waiting. I think that's the Navy's favorite place to leave you . . . hurry up and wait!

Thankfully we didn't have to wait more than a few days to receive the written, permanent hard copy orders. *Finally*, it was official and time to get all our ducks in a row for the move.

There are times in life that six months doesn't feel like a long time, like watching your babies grow. Then there are others when it feels like forever, like during deployment or waiting to hear where you're moving next. Finally, after waiting what seems like forever but was actually only about six months of riding a roller coaster of emotions month after month, the ride ended and it was time to get off. Now it would be time to prepare for what would come and the next roller coaster that came with moving.

• • •

This last round of orders, more than any time before, my emotions got the best of me. I think I had been trying to push it aside for so long that when we finally received word, all I could do was cry. Cry out of relief. Cry out of sadness. Cry out of releasing all the weight of the wait. Cry out of excitement.

Getting word you are heading back to a duty station you've been before is a bit of a bittersweet feeling, for me it was at least.

If you go back thinking life will be as it was when you were there before, you will most likely be surprised and even disappointed that is in fact *not* the case.

People who were there before have come and gone. People and relationships have changed, kids have grown up. Friendship group dynamics changed. The area may even look a little or a lot different, depending on growth.

Although you are headed back to what's somewhat familiar, there is still a bit of starting over and that's the piece I am not looking forward to. Remember that comfort zone, this is having to live outside that and I'm not a fan, but I know that God will grow me and it's part of becoming the person I am meant to be.

The focus has now gone from the waiting to hear to the waiting to move and in the meantime figuring out where to live all over again. Do you buy? Do you rent? Do you live in base housing? If only we could see the future!

You thought finally finding out where you were headed to next would mean less stress and worry? *Wrong*! Now it's a matter of figuring out timing of the packers, preparing the current house for move out, applying for housing or spending way too much time on Zillow house hunting, planning the road trip, getting the kids enrolled in a new school, searching for a new job for you, and . . . the list goes on. Somehow it all always comes together and works out, but definitely not without stress and anxiety. And sometimes not getting fully ironed out until the very last minute.

This most current move for us has been one of many lessons learned. Lessons you'd think I learned from the first, second, or even third time we've done this, but no! Perhaps I'm a little hardheaded?

One of the biggest lessons from this move is finding out more than six months before a move is so much time. So much time in the sense that there is no need to stress, yet I still am guilty of it. It may not seem like much time, but with a move, there is only so much preparing you can do that far out. You can't pack up boxes yet, you can't buy a house yet (if that's your plan), you can't do too much of a deep clean yet without having to do it again. So, the lesson I've been reminded of in all of this has been to live in the present moment. There is still work to do and blessings to come up until the time you drive away for the last time. Enjoy those moments!

You may feel the upcoming move looming over you, but can I encourage you a little? The move will still come no matter what, so long as the Navy doesn't have other plans, but that's a story for another day. There will be things that need to be done, but enjoy where you are and be present these last few months. Make those last memories with friends you hold so dear. Go out and explore the places you love close by. Cross off the bucket list items you made for this time at this current duty station. You will have time to enjoy the new place when you get there. You can't do it now.

This for me has been huge. We have been ready to leave Lemoore since the day we got here. It's not the community I don't love, but rather the place. It's a "Master Jet Base" they say, but it certainly doesn't live up to that title as far as amenities and such. The air quality is awful, it feels as hot as the sun far too much of the year, and we are a good drive from the best of activities. I have to be reminded that each new duty station comes with its own sets of pros and cons. Living here in Lemoore and getting closer to retirement has had me thinking of where we finally put down our roots. I want to absolutely love where I live and I'm not sure I've lived in that place yet.

While Lemoore might not (I'm afraid to say never) be the place we find ourselves settling down for the long haul at the end of our time in the Navy, it doesn't mean great things haven't happened here. God shows up wherever you go and, knowing your needs before you do, gives you just what you need. As I talked with another friend I met while in Lemoore, who has also moved out of the area, she commented on how hard it was to believe a place you once hated could feel so much more like home than you ever imagined, especially once you leave.

The one word that stands out to me more than any other when I think about a new duty station, whether it's a place you are looking forward to or dreading, a place you've been before or not, in order to make the most of your time there and be blessed by all God has in store, is to *flourish*!

Flourish, by definition, is to thrive, to grow, to succeed!

Think about where you are right now and answer this question: Are you *flourishing*?

I'm here to tell you, wherever you are, even if it's not your favorite location or even season of life, you can still flourish. A huge part of flourishing for me is looking around and finding those things you can be grateful for about where you are right now. It might not seem like it, but they are there. Stop and think for a minute. How many things can you come up with? It doesn't have to be all major moments, but the little ones too. They all matter.

One of my favorite things about Lemoore is the *community*.

One morning, Lucy and I had an opportunity to serve, alongside other members of the community, by picking up trash around the base. It's amazing, when you have a bag and are looking for it, how much trash people throw on the ground. It's also heartwarming to see all the people who answered the call to come out and help create a better community. I am so thankful for the team that put this together and those we ran into while picking up.

As we were out that day, I thought about where we were, in this place we didn't love, yet I felt like we were flourishing. We could so easily have arrived in Lemoore, made the choice to stay close to home with closed doors, AC running non-stop (because it gets *hot*!) and pass the time together closed off to all the opportunities and amazing people around us.

Homeschooling, a huge blessing to us, has allowed us to meet new friends, but can also lead to and maybe even encourage us to become hermits if we aren't careful. It takes work and vulnerability to step out. While it may be hard at first, it's well worth the reward.

Instead of choosing to live life feeling alone, all the while being surrounded by people, we decided to step out into the uncomfortable, even though that feeling of starting over at each new duty station is never easy.

It is by the grace of God and the love, support, and wisdom of these new friends that we find joy where we are. Through connection with others, we have also learned about many opportunities to get involved in that have in turn blessed our family, making this place we don't love one that we will certainly miss when we move.

So, to those of you who are in a place where you're struggling because you don't know anyone, family isn't close by, you don't necessarily love the area, and the easiest thing to do is feel sorry for yourself and become a hermit . . . can I just encourage you to step out, get plugged in and meet the amazing people around you? I promise there will be great joy and new friendships. Will it be as easy as it sounds? It never is. Just because it's simple doesn't mean it's easy. Is it worth it, however? *Yes*, a million times over.

I love this sound advice I once heard that went something like this, if you're sad about what you're missing, you'll miss what's right in front of you.

I thought about it for a minute and realized how true this was. How often do you find yourself looking into the future, waiting for what is to come (new duty station, new job, new season, etc.) and forgetting to enjoy what's right in front of you? Or how about comparing yourself to others and wishing you had that?

I'd be lying if I said this wasn't me often while we were in Lemoore and waiting on orders that were a guaranteed ticket out, but now as we are in the final months preparing to leave, the list of those things I am going to miss is long, so much longer than I ever imagined.

And speaking of the getting closer and closer to this move happening, I feel a bit like there is a calm before the storm. I told you earlier it's easy to stress (I do it every time too) about waiting for word on orders and then feeling like you have so much to do, yet it's too early to do anything other than enjoy where you are and wait for the move to come closer into view.

I am currently writing this as we are about two months away from our move. It's almost like nesting when you're pregnant, that buildup of what's to come and you're trying to stay as prepared as you can. Yet, here I sit in my house with no boxes packed and all looks normal. I so badly want to start the process but there is still too much time, and I'm not living out of boxes any longer than I have to.

As the time left leading up to a move becomes less and less, for me this go around, it feels too easy, too calm, like there must be a major storm brewing. I'm trying to hold it together and not stress about all I know will need to be done the closer we get and yet I think subconsciously I'm feeling the weight of the stress and the long to-do list. Maybe I'm just pretending everything will be okay. It's my coping mechanism, perhaps.

Moving day is rapidly approaching. As much as I try to not think about it, it's now in the front of my mind *all the time*! How can it not be when there are things that need to get done and planning that needs to be taken care of so the process goes as smooth as it can be. Truthfully though, smooth is not really a word I would use to describe any move!

With time in Lemoore waning, the days left much fewer, my anxiety does what it does best and starts to rear its ugly head. I suddenly feel hit with all the things that need to get done and the amount of time to get them done, but yet some things you still can't do. No matter how much you try to be prepared, to get stuff done ahead of time, it will always come down to the long list of to-dos needing to be done with a little bit of time. The good news: somehow, someway, you find a way to get it done. So today, I am choosing to live one day at a time and take on only what needs to be done on this day, a good motto for all things in life.

• • •

This time, it's not you that's moving, but a good friend. You long to help in some way. You tell them, "If you need anything, let me know! I am happy to help!" I know the intentions behind this are good, but if you're anything like me and many of my friends, we struggle asking for and taking help. Behind my struggle is the feeling of burdening others with my problems. I feel bad asking for help, even though I desperately know it's much needed.

With a move, one of the most helpful things someone can do for me and my family is invite us over for dinner or bring us a hot meal in that last week before the move.

Your kitchen is packed up, the pantry is bare, and you're dreading another night eating out, especially when the close options are McDonald's and other fast food. On your drive to wherever it is the Navy is sending you, you'll be eating fast food again. Once you arrive at your new duty station with a house full of boxes and still empty pantry, wondering where in the world all your kitchen utensils are, it would be wonderful to eat a home-cooked meal. Let's not forget to mention you're exhausted from the move and the whole process itself—cooking is the last thing on your mind.

So, if you're looking to help a friend who is moving or maybe even just moved in, fill their bellies with yummy food and some quality friend time. I promise you it will mean the world!

• • •

Okay, can we just talk housing for a moment in this whole move process?

Excitement about a move and new adventure quickly fades when I stop to think about housing. Where are we going to live? The fear is real because it seems at almost every duty station, the waitlist for housing is long, there is *no* guarantee there will be a house available when you get there, and if there isn't, who knows how long it will be until one is.

When it was just David and I, it didn't feel like such a big deal.

We didn't need much, schools didn't matter, house size didn't matter either, and just the two of us could live in a hotel for an extended period of time. But now we have two children in tow, not to mention a giant dog, along for this ride. Space matters. Location matters. Having a place nailed down to live matters.

If you haven't experienced a military move, you may be thinking, "But they provide housing or give you money for housing. Surely it's all good." It sounds that simple, but it's not at all. Ask almost any military spouse and I'm sure they'd agree that finding housing tops their moving stress list.

Let me back up for a minute. We are grateful that housing is an option—and if not housing, a housing stipend—but there's a good chance it's not quite what you think. The military provides housing, yes, if there is room and it's available for your family size and rank. As of late, there hasn't been availability, which leads to a whole new dilemma and a lot of stress.

Okay, well the solution seems easy enough. There's no room for you on base, so find a house to rent, or live out in town. There is freedom living off base, and for me, I prefer it because I don't feel as trapped or surrounded by the military. I know that sounds bad, but if you lived it you'd know you need that separation. Living off base, you now have so much to consider—do you rent, do you buy, what town, is it in a good school district?

In our current PCS (permanent change of duty station), and all the ones with our kids, it's been a major stressor, worrying and wondering whether we will have a house for us when we get there or not.

This go around we were told it could be up to seven months before a house opens up. I don't know about you, but not knowing if I will have a house right when we get there is stressful, but thinking about it possibly being seven months, that's insane (and unacceptable, in my opinion). Not to mention that's already a good portion of your time at that duty station, depending on how long you're there. Time at a duty station can range from nine months to six years. Let's be real, who wants to move more than you already have to, not to mention living in a hotel with your family circus and none of your own belongings?

For this duty station, we didn't have much choice but to go look at places out in town. Rent is not an option! The rental market is slim and rent is high, much higher than the housing allowance. I'd much rather pay a mortgage and earn equity in a home than pay rent and throw my money in the trash. Okay, so maybe that's a little dramatic.

As we continued to navigate the possibilities for housing, we were leaning towards buying, but being out of state, it makes it a bit difficult to go house hunting. You know how sometimes when you're trying to do something and you consistently get pushback, no matter what option you try, you start to question if you're making the right decision? Yes, this is exactly what happened to us.

I racked my brain, trying to explore every option possible to get myself or the family up to look at houses and each time I would strike out. It appeared physically going to look at a house wasn't an option. Have you ever considered buying sight unseen? I said I *never* would. That word *never*, coming back to bite me yet again because here we are, in a bit of a pickle.

Panic started to overwhelm me. I knew pictures online only told part of the story and usually the story that wanted to be seen, not the one that didn't. I have no doubt God was working in me, reminding me to *trust*! I had to trust that we would find housing, trust it would all work out, and trust it would be good.

There are times in life when you get pushback and realize it's most likely a sign that something is not going to work, and then comes the opposite, when things that seem impossible all start to flow together.

Things started to all work together and fall into place, beginning with our loan pre-approval. The house we loved was on the market, and we knew we wanted to put in an offer. It was still early, so I was hoping we could wait and the house would stay on the market. For some reason, on a random day, I picked up my phone and contacted our realtor, letting him know we found a house, and was wondering if he could do a walk-through with a friend, or even a FaceTime walk-through.

"Sure! I can do it today." Today? It felt so fast, but later that day I learned there was already an offer on the house, so if we really wanted the house we would have to act quickly. This upped my anxiety level. We'd looked for a few months at houses, and this was the only one we both seemed to love.

We pressed forward and did the video walk-through. The walk-through went well and we decided we wanted to put in our offer, even though it was early and we would most likely close before we arrived, but there was a problem. We hadn't received our pre-approval paperwork from the bank. So, at 4:30 pm on a Friday, we crossed our fingers, called the bank, and tried to figure out where it was. To our surprise, the person assigned to our loan was still in the office. She was able to complete the paperwork and email it off. In our offer went!

The next day was nerve-racking. If you've ever bought a house, I'm sure you know the anxiousness of waiting. We didn't know what the other offer on the table was, and we had asked that the sellers respond to our offer within the next 24 hours, because an open house was coming up and we weren't about to get into a bidding war. My heart pounded when our realtor called the next day with news. The sellers wanted to negotiate a few things in our offer and, if we made the changes, there was a good chance they would accept. I wanted to backpedal. Wait, are we sure this is the house we want? Are we sure we can afford it with a housing allowance that doesn't come close to matching the cost of our mortgage? Is the house really in good shape?

David is always my sense of reason and is able to calmly look at all sides of things. Together we decided we were going for it, moving forward even though it felt scary, even with so much unknown, and even though we had never physically walked through the house.

The inspection went smoothly, asking for fixes went smoothly, and the closing process did as well. Everything was coming together; there was no question God had his hand in it.

At this point, I still prayed that orders wouldn't be changed because, in the back of my mind, I knew that was possible *and* it had happened to us not just once, but *twice* before. In my heart, I knew I couldn't fully relax until David checked into his new command.

Closing day came, and we celebrated from California. The house was ours but now it would sit empty until our time in Lemoore was up. I'm happy to know I have a place to live. I love the house, but the process, while all things fell into place quite well, was hard. It's been incredibly expensive, and like I mentioned before, our housing allowance doesn't even come close to the market on Whidbey.

The military has decided to put blinders on and pretend that either there is nothing they can do about the shortage of housing or nothing they want to do about it. This, my friends, is so hard. It was not our choice to move—the Navy gave us orders. Do you want to know a reason why military families struggle financially? This is one of them, living in a place where housing is limited and funds meant to cover housing costs don't.

I understand it's a privilege to even get a stipend for housing, but our pay without it is minimal and nowhere near worth the hard work and time our men and women in the military put into keeping our country safe. I know I'm a bit biased, but dare I say it's a job that many take for granted.

• • •

"Are you ready for your move?"

This is a question I have been asked often, and rightfully so, when a move is in the near future, but to be honest, I'm never really sure how to answer it.

Was I excited to be back home and closer to family? *Yes!*

Was I excited to be breathing much cleaner air and see the rain? *Yes!*

Was I excited to be in a familiar area and see friends I've missed for the last three years? *Yes!*

Was I excited for all that God has in store for us in the next few years? *Yes*, absolutely!

I wasn't at all ready to say, "See you later," to all the wonderful friends I had. I was not ready for the cold. Let's just be real here, you acclimate to the warm weather real quick and it would take time to get used to the cold again. I was not packed—not a thing was in a box. I was not ready to say goodbye to our church family, who has loved on our kids and built a solid foundation in their lives. I was not ready to say goodbye to the activities our kids were involved in, to Bible study and small group. I knew the kids were not ready to say, "See you later," to their friends either. I wasn't ready to be so far from Disney, my happy place! I wasn't ready for the unknown, even though there would be so much known. I was not ready to be in the uncomfortable that would undoubtedly come.

Whidbey Island had been home before, yes, but we would be silly to think life hadn't changed since we left. It's like that deployment curve. Everyone there has continued down the straight line, and we'd be riding the rainbow curve, jumping back in having missed all the in between. I was also not ready for deployment to come, which was practically a guarantee with sea duty.

Perhaps this is how you start to feel at the end of any duty station. There are things you will miss and things you will look forward to.

My heart was ready to be out of Lemoore, because the area, as you can tell from my story, was *not* my favorite, but the blessings there had been abundant and even though we knew our time there would be short, we dug in roots—not just surface level, but deep.

One morning during worship, it hit me like a freight train that our move was approaching quickly. Dare I say this moment comes every time you move. I felt the tears well up in my eyes. I don't do "see you laters" well at all! I didn't count how many Sundays we had left, or even the total days we had left because it made it all too real and I'd just rather take each day as it came, making a to-do list and checking things off one day at a time.

This move, along with all the others, was so bittersweet. There was excitement of a new adventure, but also the hard reality of leaving so many things that we loved. I knew there would be so many blessings to come so all I could do was hold onto that hope as the sadness of leaving threatened to overtake me.

• • •

Somehow with each move, it seems to become more and more difficult. Maybe I'm more stuck in my ways. Maybe I know enough from past experiences, but I dread all that is to come. Maybe it's this and so much more. My ability to handle these moves with grace . . . well, the jury is still out. I no doubt have had my moments, many of them. Yes, I know that my attitude towards the move can determine how it goes, in my mind at least. It takes daily work to see the snippets of gratitude sometimes in the middle of this beautiful military mess.

Life feels like it's put on hold a bit during the move. I forget how much things are thrown off and how long it takes to get back to normal, whatever normal is for that moment or season.

You tell people you're moving, and they think (or even say out loud), "Oh that sounds so fun! What an adventure!" My response, "Oh it's an adventure for sure, but I don't think *fun* is the word I'd use."

It's much more than what seems to be the simplicity of movers coming to pack up your stuff and driving them to your new home.

The feeling of living in chaos with a move begins the first day the movers come with all the boxes. They move fast and by the end of the day, as you look around your once full-of-life house, you're left with empty walls and towers of boxes stacked in the corners of each room.

The weight of cleaning all the things feels a bit like a burden amongst all the other things to get done. The cleaning list seems forever long: the blinds, window tracks, lights, floors, bathrooms, kitchen, garage, and backyard. All the while, you're trying to hold it together, make sure your kids are occupied and that you don't leave anything behind.

It takes on average only two days for all of your belongings to be packed up in brown boxes and taped shut. If you forgot to pull anything out you wanted for the next short bit, it's too late now.

The truck arrives to load up all your belongings. Another step to this whole process of no longer calling this place home. This last go around, I knew it was bad news when a box truck versus the actual moving truck and driver came to load us up.

I didn't want to say it out loud and jinx anything, but this box truck meant more handling of our things. It meant sitting in a warehouse, which we learned would be more than just a day or two.

When your stuff doesn't arrive when expected and it's the holiday season, there's not much you can do, but be thankful you packed a small U-Haul trailer with some things to get by. You'd think after the many years the military has been around, and the amount of times they've moved people, it would be a well-oiled machine. Can I just tell you, it's *not!* It's a rough process every single time. You start to realize how important family is over all those things in these moves. Life, while a bit challenging because we aren't used to not having everything at our fingertips, is so simple.

Even with the realization that our things aren't *that* important, watching the truck pull away with everything causes my anxiety to rise, worrying whether all our things make it and in one piece. The wait for household goods feels long, especially when it is extended two weeks past expected. I guess the saying "expect the unexpected" was very true here for us.

My excitement returned for a brief moment when our household goods arrived. There was hope life would go back to "normal," but the process of unpacking all the things that fit so perfectly in the last house is a daunting task. But separate from your things, *you* are trying to find your place, trying to have the courage and vulnerability to put yourself out there to make new friends, not just for you, but also for your kids. You are also trying to figure out where services and stores are located, and where to go for medical and urgent care.

Nothing seemed to be going smooth this move. Nowhere did we seem to catch a break. So, wouldn't it be fitting that right after arriving, before David went back to work and checked us into medical, there would be an injury requiring a doctor's visit. After hours, on the weekend.

While exploring in the backyard, and doing what boys do best, Owen decided to hang from a tree branch. Not long after lifting his feet off the ground to let the tree hold his weight, the branch snapped. Owen fell backwards, hitting his head on a rock. He stood in the kitchen crying while David and I, in a panic, tried to figure out where we could take him that insurance would cover.

The process is overwhelming and can only be mastered one day at a time, giving thanks for good things, even if they are small.

Each morning, shortly after you arrive at your new duty station, you wake up with a to-do list of all that you dream to accomplish in that day. The list at first feels long. There is so much to do, so many things you can't find. You long for a daily normal again. It will come, but it will take time, and possibly more than you hope.

After a few weeks, you find yourself feeling settled in and it's all feeling like home once again. You're making your way around and maybe have met a few people. But the move process still isn't over.

Say what? I know, after a month, I am so ready to not be thinking about the move anymore, but chances are you have claims to file and then it's back to waiting for it all to be settled. This is a reality far too often because things get broken and go missing, especially when, like us, your stuff ends up in storage at a warehouse unexpectedly.

It seems as though the move continues to be never-ending. Settling in is slow. Not the house, but getting your bearings, finding a solid routine, and figuring out how you plug in to everything, including finding that tribe of people you can count on, because more than likely, family isn't close by.

Sitting here writing this section this morning, I feel like I am right at the heart of this unsettledness. I'm struggling to plug in, I miss the old, and would argue that the first few months, maybe longer, you find yourself in a bit of depression.

It can be so hard to let go of the old, to stop from looking back and keeping your eyes focused on what is ahead.

· · ·

Just in case you were wondering, or if you thought I seem to handle all this move stuff with so much grace, let me dispel that right now and tell you I've had more than my fair share of moments where my frustration level reached its maximum. There was anger and sadness, and days where my attitude and even my ability to speak positively just weren't my best.

I'd be lying if I said I wanted to move again, at least because of the Navy telling me I have to. I'd much rather the next move be ten or more years down the road, when the kids have graduated and David and I get to decide where we want to finally retire and put down our roots. It may be wishful thinking, but I'm not giving up hope!

Honestly though, being somewhere long term sounds a little scary and uncomfortable. What if you don't like it where you decide to make home for good? After three or four years, will we get the itch to move again? So much feels up in the air, unsettled and unknown. I'm not quite sure if our living situation will ever fully feel how I envision it in my mind to be.

· · ·

As this last Christmas and holiday season came and went, traditions have been near and dear to my heart.

Growing up, I loved all our family traditions that were wrapped up in the Christmas season. They were often the things I looked forward to most and the things that made Christmas so memorable. As David and I started our own family, I wanted that for us too—traditions.

This military life is filled with many traditions, some that are so old and outdated you wonder why they exist. While there are traditions you learn and hopefully even enjoy each year because of Navy life, it can be a bit challenging to have traditions of your own. The hardest ones are when they revolve around doing things around the place you have currently dropped anchor and call home.

This year we were in the middle of a move during the holiday season, which meant there were no Christmas decorations up, and not much time to do those things we've done in years past. This move has really made me rethink what *tradition* means for our family.

Traditions are one of my favorite things about Christmas. I remember many of the things our family did every year when I was a kid that made Christmas the incredible season it was. Many of them I want to do with my family too, but the way they look each year might be different, due to our season of life in the military.

Going to look at Christmas lights will be in a neighborhood or a light display that's mostly likely new each year.

Going on a steam train might only be in certain locations.

Our traditions will have to be more of those things you can take with you wherever you go, with being together as the most important piece. Thankfully, Lucy and Owen don't complain, which allows me to still have that special feel about traditions.

As I'm sure you know, military kids learn how to go with the flow. Each year you make new memories, starting new traditions at the duty station you are at, or getting to let the old ones play out.

• • •

Besides housing, which probably ranks at the top of my list, another big stressor during a move is knowing, unless I want to be alone, I'll be starting over with friendships.

I never wanted to be the new girl in school and was lucky to be in the same school district for the majority of my education because making friends is hard. You have to put yourself out there and be vulnerable. As adults we have many more life experiences and walls we've built up that make stepping out challenging. Sometimes ignorance really is bliss.

Let's dive deeper into friendship and community in the next chapter.

SIX

STRENGTH IN NUMBERS— COMMUNITY

Friendship with military families and civilians (those not in the military) are the community that give us life during those times we are far from family, when our spouse is deployed, and during the many different seasons and stages of life we walk through.

There are so many aspects of military life that are arguably the hardest. I'm not even sure they can be ranked. One of those hard things, at least for me anyway, is to build and then lose your tribe. These are the people you become close with, who pick you up when you're down, encourage you along the way, support you when your spouse is deployed, and listen when you need a confidante.

I feel in the trenches of this struggle right now. I never would have thought it would take me over nine months—nine—to find my place and my people, but it is.

I've been hurt by friendships in the past and so I find myself only peeking around the wall I've built. In my mind, this wall is protection, but in all reality, it's blocking the good from coming in too.

Sometimes at a duty station, you struggle to find that friend or few friends you connect with on a deep level. You know, those friends who become like family, the "2:00am friends." Perhaps you know this duty station is temporary and you just can't bear to dive in deep only to know that you will all to soon be separated from all that you put your heart into over the last few years.

Eventually, the Navy life takes over and you become separated from those dear friends, the ones you knew you could count on. I would be lying if I said the majority of my friends I call on the most in times of need are close by, because after all the moves, they are miles and miles away.

In some ways, I feel like I haven't let go of the friends who aren't local, still counting on them for as much as I can. Or maybe it's more that I'm still holding on to *what* I had before. I want that again and in desiring that special tribe I had, I feel afraid to be vulnerable in opening myself up and put myself out there again. Perhaps this is holding me back and why I'm still stuck feeling alone. The older I get the less I want to put myself out there. I'm tired—tired of starting over with friendships.

I know better than to think things will be the same as they were somewhere else. I know better than to think the friendships I had at this duty station will look and feel the same as they were before, not necessarily in a bad way, but different nonetheless. I know better, and yet I still fall into the trap of thinking it will be easy. Oh, how I wish it was!

There is this awesome thing, though! In the meantime, as we start to build and grow new friendships, we don't have to lose the old. Technology and the ability to keep in touch via text, voice, and video has made saying, "See you later," and staying in touch more bearable. There's nothing more comforting and day making than getting a message from those closest to your heart, yet miles away. A simple smile and hello from afar is sure to leave you with a smile too!

I would even argue that some of my friendships have grown stronger across the miles. Because we can't just bump into each other at the commissary or around town, it takes much more effort and time to stay connected. I am forever grateful.

• • •

Wallowing in my sadness, I spent some time talking to a dear friend from our previous duty station. Her answer to me was so simple and she totally called me out. (I'm so thankful and love her for that!) "What do you tell others to do when you're in this situation of feeling lonely?"

Ugh! I knew what that meant. It meant putting myself out there or continuing to feel so alone. See, she's exactly why I need her and other friends in my life!

But why did it feel so hard this time? I'm seasoned at this whole thing, right? I may be seasoned, but I can't say it gets easier, at least not for me. Friends, no matter how long you've been doing it, the transition and rebuilding or starting new friendships is hard. There's no sugarcoating it. I'm not sure I have the answer yet for why this time feels so much harder, and I'm not quite sure I ever will. All I know is I'm a work in progress and perhaps writing this is just what God intended for me to share with you, so you don't feel alone in this new friendship struggle.

No matter how many times you've done it, or how seasoned you are, starting over with friendships takes time, and usually longer than you want. Finding and building new friendships is just like dating. It takes time to feel one another out, to see if it's a good fit, and to hopefully make a strong connection. I do know this though, there's value in quality over quantity here.

I was recently asked, "How do you make new friends?" and it's been on my mind now since I was asked. You'd think as adults we'd have this down because we've had plenty of practice to meet new people and make new friends, yet I think with life experience this actually gets harder. Would you agree?

As a military spouse, whenever you move to a new duty station, even if it's one you've been to before, you are like the new kid in class. You don't know anyone, or the dynamic of the friendships you had have changed since you left and came back, and you find yourself trying to find a place to fit in. It's hard, it's uncomfortable, and sometimes you strike out.

Sometimes you have to go out and try some new things, new groups, new activities. Not every activity or every person you meet is going to be for you, and that's okay. Don't let that discourage you because as you continue to put yourself out there, you start to find that place where you feel most comfortable, those people who have similar values and hobbies, your people.

• • •

Get involved! Plug into the community!

How often do you hear these things when you move to a new duty station? And how hard is it to put yourself out there to meet new friends? You all know how I feel about it.

The struggle is real, wouldn't you agree? Some of you maybe even roll your eyes when you hear it, you tune it out, and just keep moving. Don't worry, you're not alone, because I have too.

But, I know better! We need people in our lives. We need relationships, good quality ones. I have learned in life that relationships are hugely important to success and joy but also require a ton of vulnerability. I bet you thought once you married your spouse you'd never date someone again, yet here you are each new duty station, "dating," instead this time it's trying to find great friends, not a spouse.

I am reminded of these verses from Ecclesiastes 4:9-12:

> Two are better than one, because they have a good
> return for their labor: If either of them falls down,
> one can help the other up. But pity anyone who
> falls and has no one to help them up. Also, if two
> lie down together, they will keep warm. But how
> can one keep warm alone? Though one may be
> overpowered, two can defend themselves. A cord of
> three strands is not quickly broken.

It's such a struggle to move to a new duty station, or even one you've been to before, and find your place. I want it to be easy. I want people to come up to me who haven't seen me before and want to get to know me. I want to be invited to join other mommas. I want to be known without having to do any work. The reality of those things happening is few and far between. *You* have to put yourself out there and be vulnerable. *You* have to look for groups to get involved with. Knowing what to do may be so simple but taking action on that knowledge is a battle, and if you're anything like me, there's some pushback. I totally get it. I am stuck there too, and this isn't the first time.

Moving forward, perhaps we shall focus on what there is to gain instead of what has been lost. The time at any one duty station can be short. Arriving, the time may seem long, but you'll blink and it will be gone. I've learned this the hard way far too many times. Unless you make the most of your time as quick as you can, you won't feel settled in with other people until the end of your tour. Don't wait!

Can I encourage you? I say you but really, I need the encouragement myself. Find a group that fits you, your life, your season, your passions. There are all kinds of groups out there: playdate groups, MOPS, Bible studies, mom groups, fitness groups (i.e., stroller warriors), command groups (Family Readiness Groups), and so much more. Whatever it is you enjoy, there's bound to be a group for you. May these groups be a springboard to finding your people right where you are. Now for myself, I need to find the group for me too!

I'm sure you, just like I do, value friendship deeply and know the importance of having people around, yet build a wall around yourself that lets little in and not a whole lot out. I've been crushed by many a friend in the past and my ability to let my guard down and trust is hard. I'd be lying if I said I have a lot of friends. I think there are many "friendships" but they're superficial. It's one of those things where you can be surrounded by people and feel alone. Have you ever experienced that?

Some duty stations are easier than others to break down those walls and start building relationships. Community and friendship groups were strong in Lemoore. There were many groups to be involved in, people constantly outside, and loads of activities held in housing, giving everyone lots of excuses to meet and talk to people.

Leading up to our move to Lemoore, I prayed hard over the friendships I would build there. I prayed for a group of ladies to love me as I am, encourage me, and lift me up. I found that in MOPS. I walked in that first day knowing no one and walked out with the beginnings of some incredible friendships that, because of the military, are separated by proximity but remain connected across the miles.

• • •

I'll never forget my first "community event." David and I were engaged. He just left for deployment and was part of a small group of people in his command sent out as support for another command. We were outsiders, had no support group, and as you know, I was a giant ball of tears and anxiety. I needed something!

Somehow, I was connected with the FRG of the command David was out supporting.

It was our first meeting. I made a forty-five-minute drive to Whidbey Island, got lost in housing (directions and maps get so confused!), but finally arrived. Late!

I entered the house to find it packed with people. It was standing room only, so I found a place in the hall beside another woman. I quickly noticed that she was with a very young baby. My heart suddenly ached for her, knowing this baby's first months of life would be without his daddy. In my head, I told myself, I would *never* have a baby while David was gone. Nope, no way! Perhaps this was the beginning of God preparing me for what I had no clue was coming, but He did, and you already read about how it all worked out.

Finally, the other woman and I struck up a conversation. It was an instant connection. Oh, thank goodness! I think at that moment I finally gave a sigh of relief for the first time since David left. We chatted, I asked how old her baby was, we shared a little about our sailors, and must have exchanged phone numbers.

Every event during deployment from then on out, we were together. We got together outside the events too, sharing our frustrations, sadness missing our spouses, and dreaming of homecoming. I remember her telling me that her countdown was how many garbage days left, which was so much smarter than counting every single day. Remember that countdown chain I did on one of David's first detachments that caused me to be miserable? I learned so much about being a great military spouse from this dear friend, Nicole.

It was a long six months, almost seven months . . . 206 days to be exact, but who was counting? The day finally came for our sailors to return.

Nicole and I met in the hangar, bundled up in our jackets, nervous about seeing our husbands again. She was nervous about how her baby, who was a momma's boy, would react to seeing his daddy again. We had tissues on the ready and waited anxiously.

Lining the front of the hangar, we stood and watched as the

plane pulled up, waving and cheering. The sailors started coming off the plane. Frantically, I was looking for David. I thought surely at 6'3" he would be easy to spot. That's not the case when they all look identical in their matching uniforms.

Nicole saw Gary and took off. I kept searching and searching the crowd. Finally, there he was! It was at that moment a sense of relief and peace overcame me and I was back in his arms once again, feeling whole.

There is nothing like the butterflies of homecoming and the feeling of being wrapped in each other's arms again. At times, the excitement and feel-good moment almost seems worth it . . . then you are reminded of how much they missed and what it was like doing life alone.

Nicole was my first military spouse friend. She encouraged me through that first deployment, greeted me with coffee early in the morning when I had to drop David off for the next deployment, and has continued to encourage me. We've both been doing this Navy life for fifteen plus years and it's such a joy to say that we are still friends, encouraging one another through life. We may be at different duty stations, but that doesn't mean the friendship ends. There is no one else I would rather have by my side and as my first friend in this military life.

The memories we share pop up at random times, and never fade away. Nicole is one of those friends you may not talk to always, but it's always picking right back up where you left off when you get the chance to talk again.

• • •

Why does it always seem like those you become closest to at any one duty station happens towards the *end* of a tour?

I would be lying if I said I wasn't a homebody (David too), and because of that, we don't get out with others or have others over enough. The places we've lived in the past have been quiet neighborhoods, where you know *of* your neighbors but don't really spend much time with them.

It's a funny thing, really. I'm not sure why it happens that way. Perhaps it's the wall of timing, knowing your time will most likely be three years or less. Why invest in something that won't be there long term? Maybe you've been burned in the past or it's simply hard work to get past the surface level friendship.

I'm living this exact thing as I write. Dear friends we've made during our tour are moving next week. We didn't get together often outside of command events, but when we did, the time we had was marvelous. There was laughter and so much joy. There was genuine care and friendship and there is just something so special about that.

I'm thankful the Navy is small and that there's a chance, however small, that our paths cross again, and our friendship picks up right where it left off.

Then it became our turn to move. As I was driving home from Bible study, I almost started to get mad at God for giving me such wonderful friendships, and yet so many of them I just started to build in the last month or so before the move. Mind you, these were friendships I even prayed for. Why would God give me these people and then just take me away from them? It's not that I want to stay in Lemoore. (I know you probably thought that.) Instead of staying, I would love to take them all with me. I joke with a good friend about having a big compound where we all live together. Wouldn't that be incredible?

Back to those newly built friendships I'm moving away from. I suppose I shouldn't look at it that way. Everything happens in God's perfect timing and I know these beautiful and amazing ladies were put into my life for a reason. Not being physically close to each other doesn't have to be the end. It can be just the beginning. Sure, it will take work to stay in touch when your paths don't cross at the commissary, NEX, church, or anywhere else in town, but I know it will be so worth the reward.

Unfortunately, there is no changing the fact that it's time to pick up and move, just when you finally felt settled in, and comfortable with your house as it is and the community you have around you. The *hope* is we can take lessons learned in building community at this duty station to the next duty station, hopefully settling in much more quickly and easily.

. . .

You did what they said to do, you dug your roots in deep and now it's time to go. You want to kick yourself for making such strong connections because it hurts to say, "See you later," to friends who have become family and dig up those roots. The friendship, with work, can most certainly endure and grow, even across the miles.

It's a blessing, this military life. You are given opportunities to move to places you may never have been able to go otherwise and maybe even never would have chosen to go. You also get to meet people and have incredible friendships you never would have known you needed. God sure shows up in more abundant ways than you could ever imagine in each duty station.

I'm thankful for all the places we've been, even though they've been hard. I'm thankful for the most amazing people I've had the privilege to cross paths with. While it's hard, like tear-jerking hard, it's such a wonderful thing to know you have friends all over the world.

In any move, know the struggle doesn't get any easier when it's time to leave those friends behind, in physical proximity anyway. I have struggled so hard, having to say, "See you later," to all my friends. As my kids get older and feel it more too, it's a struggle watching my kids go through the same.

This friendship and building community business is hard work, but at the end of the day relationships are worth it.

It feels appropriate to end this chapter with this . . .

A little note to all my friends, all of you who I've met and grown close to along this beautiful, challenging, and adventurous Navy life.

Friend, I miss you daily. Not a week goes by that I don't think of you. So many things around me bring back a flood of memories and emotions from time spent together. I know we don't talk consistently and I don't check in nearly as often as I'd like, but I promise that doesn't mean I've forgotten you!

I miss the sweet hugs from your littles. I miss the dinner get-togethers and playdates. I miss sitting on the couch, at the park, or at the pool, catching up and leaning on one another during the hard times, and good ones too. I miss running into you at the commissary, the NEX, or anywhere around town. I miss being down the street and a quick walk away. I miss all the things!

Moving away from you felt so unfair. If I had a choice, I would have either taken you with me or stayed put (depending on the duty station).

Leaving a duty station and saying, "See you later," to those precious friends you met along this last leg of the journey is incredibly hard, and it *never* gets easier! You are never quite sure if your paths will cross again, but always hope that they do. Your intentions to stay in touch are genuine, but life and time apart make it a challenge. Sometimes it feels as though your friendship is a fading memory.

Please know each of you are always in my heart and I wish we had more time together. Until we see each other again . . . Much love to you all!

SEVEN

NOT ALL SUPERHEROES WEAR CAPES—MILITARY KIDS

Strong.
Brave.
Courageous.
Loving.
Resilient.
Hero.

These are just a few of the words that come to mind when I think of Owen and Lucy, as well as every other military child.

Growing up, my parents were so present in my life. Sure, my dad traveled here and there, but never for more than two weeks at a time. Those two weeks felt forever long then, but now in military life, two weeks is a breeze! As a kid, I can't imagine saying, "See you later," to a parent for months at a time. I mean, I struggle with it as an adult and spouse, and yet somehow military kids do it and with such poise and strength. I have a lot to learn from them.

The experiences these military kids go through, other children will never have to experience. Some of the situations they face, like being without a parent for an extended period, are not at all easy, but every experience shapes them into some of the most incredible kids I know.

Just simply living military life teaches kids a variety of lessons. They learn to go with the flow, and dare I say, better than adults do. They have had to say, "See you later," for far longer and far too many times than anyone would wish for their children. It's not just saying goodbye to a parent when they leave for deployment, but to the great friendships they build at each duty station. They grow up understanding that living with one parent for an extended period time is "normal." They become great at making new friends and adapting to a new location, another skill I am often taking lessons from my kids in. They consistently remind me how to find joy in the little things, to love deeply and have faith in what you can't see.

This military life we live is far from easy. Yes, we knew when we married our service member what this life might entail, but our kids didn't have a choice of this life they were born into.

I've heard many say about military kids that they are resilient. To this I would agree but also say that doesn't mean they don't struggle. I'm realizing that saying, "See you later," never gets any easier for them either. I would even argue that it gets harder as they get older because they understand more and remember more.

• • •

One of the most challenging things as a parent to a military child are those moments you watch your kids say, "See you later," to their daddy. I am a crier all by myself, but insert kids into the equation and I'm guaranteed to be on the hot mess express.

The word "bye" is often a heavy word for military kids. There are seasons of military life, most often the ones filled with detachments, deployments, living far away from family, and people constantly coming and going enough that they feel like all they do is say "bye" to all those they love and hold dear.

Confession: because of the amount of times my kids get let down, I will wait to tell them about fun things until I know for certain they will happen. It breaks my heart every time they get let down. Perhaps I am being overprotective. I know in life disappointment happens and they have to learn how to deal with it, but I think military kids learn how to do that pretty well, so I will choose to protect them from disappointment *most* times, if I am able.

I'll never forget the day David had to leave for a short detachment. Short in military terms is usually around a few weeks. The kids were old enough to understand Daddy was going on a work trip, but not quite old enough to understand the time he would be gone.

David stepped out of the car to gather all his belongings. There is just something about a sea bag that brings all the emotions. The moment that bag comes out, the weight of time away from each other takes hold. It will always be a symbol of separation for me, not at all like luggage and the excitement of a vacation.

Walking around the car, David opened each side door to kiss and hug the kids. The second Lucy's door opened, the flood of tears erupted. Clinging to David's jacket, she begged him through her tears, "Don't go, Daddy. Don't go!"

I was crying too. My heart broke into a million pieces. She clung to David with strength I didn't know a toddler possessed. I have no doubt she thought if she just held on then he wouldn't have to go. She's not alone in wishing that would be the reality.

I can't even imagine how David feels when he leaves. Perhaps it's feelings of guilt that he has to go, even though it's his job. All I know is better him than me! My hope as he walks away, is that he always knows how deeply loved he is, and that we will be counting down until he returns.

Getting into a new routine without Daddy always takes time and teamwork. These first few days or even week or so are a transition, and one that reminds us daily that something in our life is missing.

Not a day goes by that at least one, if not both, of my kids tell me, "I miss Daddy!" My response will always be, "Me too!"

Doing the deployment for the third time with kids, I realized it doesn't get easier for them either. It helps now that they're old enough to have a better understanding of time, but they each have a special relationship with Daddy and there's a hole they feel when David is gone. It's important to acknowledge that, to talk about it, and to constantly remind them how much Daddy loves and misses them too.

To help pass the time, we stay busy, we hold each other close, and we are intentional with our time. We always take time to talk to Daddy, which sometimes means dropping everything for a moment or two. We write cards and prepare care packages to send. Even though Daddy is gone, I do my best to keep him as present in our lives as possible.

One activity we started on our latest deployment was gratitude journals. The days can be hard, especially when there is nothing more that you want then to have Daddy home, but we are learning to focus on the good too, no matter how small it is some days.

Each night, as part of our bedtime routine, the kids write or draw about one, but often more, of the good things that went on that day. This also helps us remember to tell Daddy all the important things the next time we talk to him.

During our latest deployment, things cropped up, emotional things I never would have expected. I suppose that's not too out of the ordinary with how things go on deployment. I always try to tell myself I am prepared for what will come, but anxiety and depression in the kid I never expected it from slammed into me hard.

The moment I realized what was going on, the reason the symptoms didn't make sense but then suddenly did, my heart shattered into a million pieces. I have felt the exact same way she felt. My child, who is my sidekick, felt the weight of Daddy being gone so much more than I would have ever thought or expected.

Just as much as I felt I needed therapy, it became evident how much my kids did too. Working to find each of them a therapist became priority over myself. The only problem, the same one I have been fighting for myself, is being able to find a therapist that is covered under our military insurance and has availability. You'd think in a lifestyle where life is constantly changing, you are often without one parent, and emotions are bound to run high, that mental health resources would be more readily available, but this hasn't been the case.

We are still searching for a therapist, but I am bound to break the anxiety cycle with my kids, or at least get a head start on teaching them skills to deal with fear as it arises. This is one of those times where military life is far from glamorous, and not addressed enough. I'm not sure how, but my hope is to bring it more to light, to let other military parents know they are not alone, and maybe even find a way to have resources more available.

Every day these kids amaze me with their ability to keep pressing forward. They seem to know when days are hard and the parent holding down the home front needs a little extra love. They also seem to recognize how, when the other parent is away, there are fewer eyes watching, the perfect time to test the boundaries.

With all they go through, these kids are beyond amazing. I look up to them and their strength to carry on and face each day with courage and bravery. It's nothing short of admirable. From them, I learn how to keep my head high, go with the flow, and adapt to newness and the unknown as best I can. Without a doubt, each of these kids is my hero!

• • •

Have you seen those videos circulating of all the homecoming clips? You know, the ones where the military member surprises their spouse and/or their kids. How about the ones where the service member and their dog are reunited after so many months apart? I'm always drawn into watching these and am left wiping away tears every time. Tears because I know the feelings that come with being reunited with your spouse after far too long apart. My kids have been the ones who see Daddy and take off at a full sprint to be swept up in his arms. Time on the phone and FaceTime does no justice to actually being together in person.

I will never fully understand what it's like to get Daddy back from my kids' point of view, except for the raw emotions they have and the smile you can't wipe off their faces for days to come.

For me, time spent out in the hangar waiting for David to get home is torture because that last hour feels like forever long. But for the kids—thank goodness for bubbles, bounce houses, and sugary treats.

There is nothing sweeter than your kids holding a sign you all made together, welcoming Daddy home. One of my favorite signs we made for homecoming was simple—"Best Day Ever!"

Having Daddy back in our arms truly is the best day ever, and not just the first time he came from deployment, but each time after that too.

Those first few weeks David is home, I am not nearly as needed, and you know what? I am one hundred percent okay with it. It's nice to have someone else to answer the millions of questions, to be the one whose space bubble they constantly invade, and to be the one to wipe bottoms. Don't mind me while I just find a quiet place to enjoy some much-needed alone time after all the months of constantly being "on".

● ● ●

Every three to four years involves preparing for yet another duty station change. We have not had the privilege of staying in one place for two tours back to back, but maybe that's a blessing. I'll let you decide.

Owen and Lucy are getting to the age where they remember so much and have a better understanding of things. As I watch them play with their friends, my heart aches, knowing that at such a young age they'll learn the art of saying, "See you later," to their best friends, and not just once but over and over again. Recently, while we have not been the ones to leave, we've said goodbye to some incredible friends. Not a week goes by that my kids don't bring up their friends, followed by, "I miss them, Mommy!" Their sadness of missing their friends is one I know all too well, so it breaks my momma heart big time.

As I talked to a good friend from Lemoore, Samantha, who has two kids that my kids absolutely love (and so do I), she mentioned how before we moved she waited to tell her daughter that we would be moving soon. She didn't have the heart to tell her until it was very close to our move, and I am much the same with my kids. We agreed that moving is something we don't talk about too much and tried to live each day in the present and soak up as much time as we could together. Putting a lot of emphasis on moving, in my opinion, only made it harder. Samantha also commented on how separation is a part of life that our kids have to get used to. As a mom, it's hard to know your kids will feel this pain and even have to get used to something that most other kids, even adults, don't have to learn how to navigate.

While it's hard in the moment to say goodbye, I am so thankful for the beautiful memories my kids have made with all their friends, including friends all over the world. Saying "See you later" doesn't have to mean forever. In military life, you never know when your paths might cross again. This Navy life is smaller than you think and there's a good chance we get to see some of them again, and even if the Navy doesn't bring us to the same location, we will just plan trips with our friends to our favorite places, like Disneyland and the beach. There's also the opportunity for the kids to be pen pals. Who doesn't love getting mail, especially from a special friend?

• • •

There are so many traits about my children that I love and admire, and one of those things is their ability to make friends.

You read before about community and the challenge it is for adults to learn how to and be vulnerable enough to make new friends. Did it cross your mind that our kids have to do the same? Somehow making friends seems to be a gift, or at least comes easier for our kids. I think there is a lot we can learn from our kids and their ability to do so with such ease.

Kids are willing to be vulnerable and they don't, or at least seem not to, hold judgement against others. Everyone they encounter can be a new friend.

Do you ever get jealous of how easy it is for your kids to make friends, or maybe how open they are to new friends? No, just me?

This my friends, is a blessing! Where you might have a weakness, your kids have a strength. I know we so often think that as adults we are supposed to be doing the teaching, but there is so much we can learn from our kids. Sure, our kids may sometimes be socially awkward, or make a situation uncomfortable, but would you believe me when I say many of my friends have come because my kids were willing to play with other kids at the park or talk to other adults nearby?

Our kids have this awesome innocence, with much less life experience holding them back from talking to someone new or trying something new. Use this to your advantage! I love to learn from my kids and this is one area that will not always be easy, because often I don't want to have a conversation and just want to keep to myself. They've helped me come out of my shell and blessed me with friendships I may not have ever had. God uses our kids too, especially when He knows we need it.

The kids have many opportunities to meet new people and oh, how they do! After a move, Lucy tells me after almost every new activity, whether it be children's church, choir, cheerleading, or Awana, that she has a new friend. It makes my heart full knowing they don't feel alone.

May we as adults learn from their willingness to love others and make new friends.

. . .

Recently a friend shared about military kids, and the reminder to put ourselves in their shoes. Even though we share experiences of life in the military, we don't understand everything our kids go through. I never was a military brat, so I never will fully know what it feels like to have a parent in the military.

It's easy to focus on myself and how hard I have it, but what about my kids? Sure, maybe they don't fully understand what's going on at a young age, but it still impacts them in some way. They are bound to be shaped by this military life, and hopefully in mostly, if not all, positive ways.

They too can suffer from anxiety, depression, and stress during the challenging times of military life. Think of moves—not only are they leaving their good friends, but they're moving schools, which means new people to interact with and new teachers. It can all feel so overwhelming and scary. Think of deployments and missing their deployed parent as well as the unintentional stress put on by the parent on the home front trying to cope.

These kids are truly some of the toughest I know and, while they have the ability to adapt well, let's remember how they might be feeling before we tell them to just get up and get over it.

EIGHT

WHAT ABOUT ME– LIFE AS A SPOUSE

Who are *you*? What hats do you wear?
I am a wife, a military wife.
I am a mom.
I am a homeschool mom.
I am a volunteer.
I am a friend.
I am a sister.
I am a daughter.

It's so easy to get caught up in the busyness of life, doing things for others, that you get put on the back burner. We talked about you being an anchor for your spouse and as the anchor for our families, we tend to focus on keeping *everyone* else together, which means we don't get time for some self-love and self-care.

As a military spouse, your sense of identity gets lost, or if not lost, then buried down under the piles of commitment and priorities this military life brings.

Now don't get me wrong, there is great joy and identity in being a military spouse, but that doesn't have to, nor should it be your everything. Who you were before you married your service member still matters! Marrying your spouse also means marrying the military. The military does what they do best by seemingly taking over your life, but that doesn't mean you should let go of who you are, your dreams and goals, and the person you long to be.

Will life look different than it did before you became a military spouse? Well, yes! But is that bad thing? I'd like to think it's not at all bad. Use it to your advantage.

You have a purpose. Yes, *you*! And I can bet you it's far more than being "just" a military spouse. One of your titles may be *spouse* but that doesn't mean that you can't live out your dreams, desires, and goals. Don't let your status as a military spouse define you.

Have you ever felt like, because your spouse's demanding career dictates where and when you move, it's not even *worth it* to find a job or have a career yourself? I know I have.

I *hate* interviews! I *hate* that I have to figure out if my certification in one state will transfer to the next. I *hate* that I have to fill out job application after job application and repeat this process every couple of years when we move. It's exhausting and, dare I say, defeating when the market is slim because jobs are few or the town is small.

Just because it's hard and takes a good amount of work, it doesn't mean you should give up on what you feel called to do.

As I write this section, I'm on an airplane heading to Indianapolis, without my kids, without my husband. I am going for *me*! I am going to see my friends and do what I love to do. It's exciting and it gives me purpose. It brings me joy and gives me an outlet.

Can I encourage you to find and fight for something you love, maybe a purpose you can take from duty station to duty station? Perhaps that thing will be a way that helps you step out of your shell a little when you get to a new place and allows you the opportunity to make instant friends.

We all need a little something for us because otherwise, all too easily the military consumes us and takes over *every little bit* of our lives.

As you think about the thing that fuels your fire and is for *you*, know this: It doesn't have to be a paid job. Maybe it's serving at a food bank weekly, or leading MOPS, or running a fitness club, or writing a book, or serving at church. Whatever it is, you will be surrounded by a community of others. It's like instant friends, especially if you're in a new location. That's a huge win, right?

Don't be afraid to do something for you. Sure, there are seasons where our time is focused more on our family or other things, but please don't forget about you.

Sometimes finding something that allows you to feel like you still have your own identity means stepping outside the military realm. You work off base with people who have no association with the military. If this is what you need, awesome.

Maybe you still need to be closer to military life, and that's great too. You can still find your own identity doing things military related, like volunteering to be a command ombudsman. An ombudsman is a liaison between your spouse's command and the families of that command. You get to be a resource to other families within the command.

I served in this role early on in David's military career, and while it's not one I would choose again, it was perfect for me in that season of life. The learning that came with this experience was invaluable. I learned so much about the military itself, about the command, its structure, how things were run, and it was another friendship-making opportunity.

In this process of finding and doing those things that light you up, my hope is your spouse supports you. The pushback from our spouse or anyone close to us can put a damper on things, but don't let that be the reason you stop doing for you. Eventually, after they see your joy and the hard work you've put in, they will hopefully change their mind and stand right behind you, even cheering you on.

Okay, so we talked about finding purpose for *you* but what about making the time to *take care* of *you* physically??

This is so important, my friends!

I love this image described by a good friend who spoke to our MOPS group a few years ago. She talked about how each of us each have a cup, and in that cup . . . *glitter*! Life is always better with a little bit of glitter, right? Well, maybe not! You either just squealed with excitement or rolled your eyes thinking of the mess it could make.

Anyway, with that cup, you sprinkle glitter over others when you help them—watch their kids, make a meal for them, or whatever you do for them. Eventually, what happens to that cup? It becomes *empty*. And guess what? You can't pour from an empty cup, can you? This is the stage I like to call burnout.

In this stage I start to feel agitated. Looking around it seems all I do is give and give and give, not getting anything in return. I know reading that may sound selfish, but the feelings are there nonetheless.

When these feelings begin to creep in, it's important to recognize them and then turn that cup *up*! True satisfaction is not going to come from others. We are an imperfect people and no matter how hard we try, people will not give us true lasting satisfaction, but God can. Allow Him to fill your cup back to the brim so you can regain joy in loving on others and sprinkling them with that glitter.

I have spent a lot of time in prayer as these feelings arise, just being thankful for all the people in my life. I pray for God's strength because I sure can't do it on my own.

Another thing you can do is give yourself grace in saying no sometimes. Know your boundaries and the time you have available. I know it's hard to say no. I'm a total yes girl, but there is power, energy, and joy when you allow yourself to care for you. You will have more to give in return. I have also learned the hard way that if you don't slow down, life will force you to.

•   •   •

What about fitness and nutrition? Oh, yes! Those of you who know me, know that this piece was not going to be left out.

Fitness is a passion of mine and the change it's made in all areas of my life is not something I will keep a secret.

The excuse I most often hear about this area of self-care is, "I don't have time!" Your spouse is gone and you're single parenting it. That means you're up in the middle of the night when any of the kids or dog is up. You're the one running from activity to activity and trying to be two places at once. Attending the conferences. Not to mention your own job, if you have one.

Fitness is a life-giving activity. This I promise you! You should know this about me: I was the mom who claimed to exercise three to five days a week, when I really wasn't doing any true physical activity. Want to know why? I chased two toddlers around all day, and in my mind that counted. Until the day the nurse asked (in not the nicest tone), "Does your heart rate go up?" In my best *Full House* Stephanie Tanner voice, I was thinking, "How rude!" In effort to respond and still seem like I had it all together I said, "Ummm, well . . . *Sometimes!*" It was then I realized I needed something more.

Thank goodness for friends, friends who are encouraging, and friends who have strengths where you seem to struggle.

What in the world was I supposed to do to find fitness when I had two little ones, my spouse deployed, and little motivation because I was running on empty and lack of sleep?

While the answer for some is going to the gym, that just wasn't practical for me. My kids weren't in school and our schedule was unpredictable, so trying to fit in a class at the gym just seemed more overwhelming. And what about childcare? Ugh! I was thinking, "Ewww! The germs of other kids!" Real raw truth here, kids at daycares and places like this are a struggle for me with the germs because all I see is snotty runny noses. Caring for sick kids with my hubby gone just wasn't on my top priority list. The excuses just kept coming.

Thank goodness there was something I could do at home, on

my own time, and in the quiet of my bedroom before my kids woke up. You see, they have some secret Spidey sense that alerts them to wake up when I go downstairs. So, I plugged in my DVD and went to work.

Did it always feel good? *No*, not in the moment, but afterwards it always did. That post-workout high is real! I am one of those people who enjoy being sore. Are you?

It took hard work, consistency, dedication, determination, and fight to get it done, especially on the days I didn't want to. As I continued to make this time for me, usually thirty to forty minutes four to five days a week, I started to feel better, stronger, and more confident. I even had more energy to make it through the day and keep up with my kids, who never seemed to be still, unless they were sleeping. There was also some motivation to knock David's socks off when he returned from deployment.

Positive changes were happening in areas I never imagined, more than just the scale, which I eventually tossed out. It gave me every reason to keep on trucking.

Another plus of fitness was being surrounded by a community of other people, mostly women, working on their own self-care goals. Although my workouts were done alone, I talked with these women daily online. We have become so much more of a digital world these days, but in this military life, I am so thankful I am able to keep in touch with my friends who are all over the world and even make new friends in online fit groups. These ladies have become some of my best friends.

When you're surrounded by other motivated people, you can't help but also be motivated. Oh, and guess what else, you just got some more instant friends. They may not be local, but they were there to hear your struggles and frustrations, celebrate your victories, and help pick you up when you fall.

• • •

Last but not least, let's not forget about mental health. As a military spouse, it's easy to bottle up all your emotions, the emotions that go with this military life, on top of mom life, on top of keeping up the house, work life, and all the other pressures of life. We feel the need to be strong for our kids and to show the outside world we've got this, but if you're anything like me, just continuing to push it down only adds fuel to the fire that soon will erupt.

Why is there so much shame and negativity associated with going to see a counselor or a therapist?

Over the past few months, I've tried to hold it all together, keeping in the feelings of fear, anxiety, and sadness because I feel like everyone is looking to me to be strong. The only problem is I find myself spiraling farther and farther down the hole of complete overwhelm.

I need a therapist. No, that doesn't have to mean anything is wrong. No, it doesn't have to be a secret. No, there is no shame in it, but instead perhaps bravery for being willing to be vulnerable. I'm realizing there is value in seeing a counselor when things are hard, but also when things seem to be going well.

We all have baggage and experiences we've tried to push down and ignore, but somehow they have a way of creeping back up and rearing an ugly, ugly head. Wouldn't you agree?

I encourage you to talk about it with someone you trust (a neutral party is best), someone who can listen, encourage you, and pray with you. You weren't meant to do life alone and carry burdens quietly by yourself.

You might not realize the abundance of resources available because sometimes we blind ourselves from them by telling ourselves that we are doing just peachy. I know I did! It wasn't until I was open with those around me about my need for help that I realized the abundance of resources. I bet you'll find you are not alone. Don't be afraid to ask for help, and even ask for recommendations from your friends. A dear friend reminded me that counselors and therapists were given their talents and skills to be used, and to help other people like me. So, use them!

I love this thought a sweet friend recently told me. Seeing a therapist or counselor when your mind isn't feeling well is (or *should be*) as normal as seeing a doctor when your body isn't physically feeling well.

I know it's hard to pick up the phone and call. It's hard to keep fighting against constant roadblocks. The easy solution is to give up when the fight gets harder than it already felt, but can I encourage you to keep fighting, keep calling, and keep trying.

You are *worth* it and I know you won't regret taking the time to focus on your mental health.

It's you holding down the home front while your spouse is deployed, so taking care of you is vital in order to best take care of your family and support your spouse from miles and miles away. After all, happy wife equals a happy life, right?

NINE

CONCLUDING THOUGHTS

This military life is far from easy.

Hard to you is going to be different than hard for me. In each of our lives, we will encounter hard and challenging times. I don't get to judge you and your hard just like you don't get to judge mine. Despite the hard that comes in this military life, and in your life too, if we let the challenges give us reason to make excuses for why we continue to be trapped by our circumstances, life will be miserable.

You can indeed find joy, strength, intention, and grace through the hard. While it will be a battle, life can be much more enjoyable than staying stuck in the hard.

Identify your hard. Say it out loud and bring it to the light. Take power out of the struggles weighing you down and start thinking of a solution to work towards overcoming it. Surround yourself with others who will encourage you and cheer you on.

Choose to show up daily and be consistent, following the steps you know you need to take and overcome the hard. I can promise when you do, you will begin to see the blessings out of the chaos and even find gratitude in the hard you're living. Now that sounds worth it, doesn't it?

Life is full of adventures, trials, and the unexpected. Each day there are many opportunities to take those things on with grace and with intention. Will it always be easy? *No*! Some days will prove to be much more challenging than others. Those days are not days to be viewed as failure or disappointment, but ones to learn from and try again the next time something similar arises. While not every moment is a good one, there are always good moments if you seek them out.

I don't have this military life figured out, and know I am probably nowhere close to mastering it, even after the fifteen years I have worn the hat of military spouse. I'm not sure I ever will have it fully figured out. The military is always great at throwing curve balls just when you thought you knew what you were doing. Nothing like keeping you on your toes!

The experience of being a military spouse has taught me so much and has helped form me into the person I am today. I'd like to think I've gained a lot of grace and managed much better over time and experience.

You never know what each day will bring in this military life. You could think everything is planned out and the next minute be told your move was sooner than you thought, or maybe that your move is now to a new location, or perhaps that your spouse is leaving sooner or coming home later than you expected.

I do believe it is possible to take on each day with joy in your heart and grace to handle the challenging moments (which will no doubt come) as best as you can.

I'm still a work in progress and continue to take each day as it comes. There's not much more you can do than that. My priority is to cherish time as a family, live with intention, and give grace in all situations, even in those moments I don't want to.

A happy and successful life is possible in the military. I know you may have had your doubts. That's not to say that there won't be hard seasons because there will be. Life isn't promised to be easy, but I can promise you great friendships will be made to last a lifetime.

You will get to enjoy experiences you might not have otherwise, and you'll no doubt have stories to tell: funny ones, heartbreaking ones, ones of courage, and ones of celebration. Hold tight onto those good times because they will give you the strength and light to press on during the hard ones. Seek gratitude daily. Write it down, so you can look back on those joyful things when you're in need of a pick me up.

I love this quote from the book *Love Lives Here*[4], by Maria Goff. She says, "Unfortunately, more often than not, we found ourselves reacting to the next big event instead of living life with intention, reason, and purpose."

I am definitely guilty of doing just that—reacting—when it comes to so much of this military life. What if we did like she said and lived each moment, went through each move, and took on deployment with those three words: intention, reason, and purpose? How would going through those seasons look and feel then?

I'm leaving this as a question and challenge not just to you, but to myself. It takes work to keep the good and positive thoughts in the forefront of our mind when the negative moments so easily try to steal the thunder.

· · ·

Some Final Takeaways

Learn to be flexible. It always feels better when you allow for change than feeling you were forced into something. We are not much different than our kids and find power in choice, even if it's "choice," if you know what I mean.

Find joy and gratitude in all the moments, especially the hard ones. Sometimes you just have to laugh at the way things play out because if you don't, it can be miserable.

---

[4] Maria Goff, *Love Lives Here: Finding What You Need in a World Telling You What You Want* (Nashville, TN: B & H Publishing Group, 2017), 212.

Give yourself grace—your spouse and your kids too. This life is not an easy one, like you've heard me say many times over. Things aren't going to go as planned, no matter if you're living this military life or life outside the military. Sometimes we need to just take a step back and breathe.

Be intentional! I mean it's in the title, right?

Lean on other spouses. We aren't a tight-knit community for no reason. We need each other.

• • •

The future is uncertain, yet we try to do everything in our power to control what will come. How many times have you planned something for the future and when the future became the present it wasn't what you expected? How many of you experience anxiety when you think ahead to the future and the possibilities of what could happen? *Me!*

Is it important to have a *vision* of where you desire to be and feel led to go? *Yes!* Is it important to set goals? *Yes!* But I believe both of these need to be done while keeping in mind that God must be included in all you imagine for the future. It's also essential not to linger in the future or planning what is to come because this is when our anxiety sprouts like weeds and threatens to take over. What is worrying about the future going to do other than make you miserable?

I have been what I like to call a "worry wart" for so long and have learned it's nothing short of crippling. I am thankful for the experiences God has placed in my life to help me realize worrying does not do any good. Marrying into the military is one of those things. Do I still worry? Oh yes, but not nearly as much as I used to, and I believe there is less worry because of my reliance on the Lord.

As you think about your future and the plans you dream of, may you remember this from Ephesians 3:20-21, "Now to him who is able to do immeasurably more than all we ask or imagine, according to his power that is at work within us, to him be glory in the church and in Christ Jesus throughout all generations, for ever and ever! Amen."

Don't forget to be present in the moment of today, not getting caught up in what might come, which is so easy to do in the military when you're stuck in the middle of military challenges. Trust in the Lord and allow Him to pave the path ahead, guiding you along the way. This is not just a challenge to you, but one to me also, remembering to seek Him in all things, both in the present and future, good and bad.

•   •   •

Our future in the military, what will it hold? Our future outside the military, what will happen then? The end seems to be drawing closer and closer, faster and faster. This is a place I always dreamed of coming and now that it's here I find myself uncertain about what's to come. This military life is all we have known. While it's a challenging life, it becomes comfortable over time. You expect the moves every couple of years. You expect your plans to be turned upside down by a last-minute change of orders. You expect deployment. Sometimes we stay in the comfortable even when it's painful because we know it and have learned to cope.

Big decisions are ahead and life outside the military is coming whether I feel ready or not. For everyone in the military, the day will come when military life is a story of the past.

David and I have been doing a bit of thinking, discussing, brainstorming, and dreaming about our future and what comes next. As I sit and think about what will come, all I can do in the moment is pray that what we do now is preparing us for what is to come.

During all the times David is gone, traveling with the military, it sparks our thoughts and desires for our future. It reminds us of our priorities, with family being number one. David being gone is hard for everyone and while the kids miss him and talk about him daily, I can tell David struggles to be away from all of us.

I'm not sure what the future holds. Will we be in longer than twenty years because we are finding joy in where we are, or is that the point we say our goodbyes and break ties with full time, active duty military? Only time will tell.

All your experiences this military life offers, both the victories and the trials, shape you into who you are. In the moment, the struggles feel hard, but looking back, you can see how they prepared you for what was to come, made you stronger, and made you into the beautiful person you are now.

While I'm sure you don't wish to walk through those battles again, I think we can all agree that there is gratitude in the blessing that walking through them has brought.

I can promise you in these next few years as we live out the life of a military family, we will do our best to make the most of each moment, hold tightly to one another, be present and live with intention, and always do our best to find joy and gratitude in each situation.

APPENDIX A

HELPFUL NEED-TO-KNOWS TO GET YOU STARTED

Disclaimer: Policies and procedures are constantly changing in the military. While you get yourself established as a spouse, you may find that some of the steps follow a little different procedure or require you to go to a different place. Some acronyms used here may not apply, or be exactly the same, in all military branches.

#1 Learn and be willing to go with the flow and always expect the unexpected.

#2 Learn the many important military acronyms. Check out the helpful resources in Chapter 2.

#3 **Don't be afraid to ask for help!**

#4 Order and obtain an extra copy of your official marriage certificate.

#5 File said marriage certificate with your personnel department, which then allows you to be entered into DEERS (Defense Enrollment Eligibility Reporting System) so you start to receive

BAH (Navy term for Basic Allowance for Housing), get an ID card, and be covered under TRICARE insurance.

#6 With a copy of DEERS paperwork and ID card, head to the hospital to enroll in TRICARE for medical insurance.

#7 Decide whether you prefer to be seen at the base hospital with TRICARE Prime or off base with TRICARE Select. Enroll in your preferred choice.

The process is still confusing to me now and can change without notice. Hopefully, at the least, this gets you started where you need to go.

APPENDIX B

HOW TO HELP OR ENCOURAGE OTHER MILITARY SPOUSES

1. Be his/her friend.

As you've read over the last hundred pages or so, I'm sure you've come to realize that this military life is hard. Maybe you even feel like it's a totally different world. If it makes you feel better, I feel that way too a lot of the time.

There is so much change happening all the time and having a friend who will listen when he/she just needs to complain about the struggle and not be judged for it, a friend who is willing to help out when there's an emergency, a friend who encourages and lifts up on the hard days, and a friend that celebrates the victories with is vital to this life. Be a friend!

2. Make a meal.

We've all had that time when life was so overwhelming that thinking about and cooking food for your family felt like too much. Cereal for dinner again? Perhaps you're trying to navigate life with a newborn and your spouse is deployed. Maybe you're healing from surgery and your spouse is deployed, again. Or possibly you're smack dab in the middle of a move, all your utensils and pans are packed, and the pantry is bare. These are the moments I know I myself as a spouse have had the privilege of receiving a meal or know it would be an incredible gesture. So, if you're wondering how to help, this is a great way.

3. Recommend a babysitter or be a babysitter.

Those of you who are parents know it's extremely difficult to find sitters you trust with your kids. Your kids are your most prized possession and you don't want to leave them with just anyone. Be willing to share the names and numbers of your favorite sitters, or even watch the kids yourself.

4. Spend time with him/her.

This military life, especially while one's spouse is deployed, can get extremely lonely, weekends in particular. A military spouse doesn't require much. I bet most times, they don't even want to ask when they're in need, but having a friend to invite them to activities on the weekend or to just come and sit with them and have adult conversation means the world.

5. Just show up.

I'm sure by now you've gathered that military spouses don't often ask for help, even when you can see they are in need. Take the initiative to help with that need, whether it be taking the kids so they can grocery shop alone, showing up at their house with a cupcake or cup of coffee, just because, or coming over to just listen and be there for conversation.

APPENDIX C
WHY I AM WRITING TO YOU

April 23, 2018

As I laid awake at 2:00 am yet again, I wondered if God was waking me up at the same time every night to speak to me. It seemed like more than just a coincidence that I was woken up at the exact same time *every* night for a week!

So, I prayed 1 Samuel 3:10. "Speak, for your servant is listening."

I had no idea what to pray for and felt like it was a shot in the dark. I flipped through ideas in my head like you flip through a Rolodex business card file looking for a name. Could it be the kids? No. The dog? No. The house? No.

It was then the idea of writing a book came to my mind. It's been a dream for quite some time and it seems everywhere I turn I hear these words, "Maybe your dream is to write a book," in which every single time my heart quietly screamed, "Yes!"

Hearing things over and over are always a sign that God is nudging me, but I've thought about what I would write about and nothing, I mean *nothing*, came to mind until this middle of the night wake up call.

God prompted me to write about navigating life through the

military, the ups and the downs, the good and the hard. I suddenly felt a tug on my heart to share my story as a way to inspire and encourage others that, while this life is hard and not everyone understands, there will be bad with all the good. Wearing the hat of a military spouse is an incredible honor and is a life filled with opportunity, so much joy, and love.

CPSIA information can be obtained
at www.ICGtesting.com
Printed in the USA
LVHW091511171120
671933LV00019B/681